Once you fix your credit the rest of your life will fall into place...

Instagram: @SchoolOfCreditRepair

www.schoolofcreditrepair.com

This book is dedicated to Jacob, Kennedi and Kameron. Thanks for motivating me to create services and self-help books to teach world the process of financial freedom. Also, to my mom, thanks for always being encouraging and my support system while I work on any project.

Congratulations! on taking it a step further to restore your credit. This Credit Repair Dictionary is a very Aggressive KIT equipped with letter templates only. Every single letter in this package has been successfully used by some of the industry's top credit repair companies and attorneys to get bad debt and accounts successfully deleted from all three major credit bureaus forever. Please browse through this book and pick out the letters that best suits your situation. Along with this guide you should've received my very first "Do It Yourself" Credit Repair Kit (eBook) via email along with 2 other eBooks. Please read those kits in entirety before browsing through this book. As always be sure to tailor each letter to your own personal situation. Most of the letters included are self-explanatory or have instructions at the beginning. If you have any questions or concerns feel free to contact my support team at schoolofcredtrepair@gmail.com. Please keep in mind; this is a very inexpensive service so please allow us time to respond to your request. There are so many free answers on my social media outlets but if you're still lost feel free to reach out to our support team.

Thanks and we wish you the best of luck on your Credit Repair Journey.

Table of Contents

                                  Page #

1. Dedication 1
2. Introduction 2
3. Table of Contents 3
4. Basic Dispute for Collections 7
5. Victim of Identity Theft 8
6. Basic Dispute for Creditor or Furnisher 9
7. Validate Debt (609 Letter) 10
8. Method of Verification 11
9. Method of Verification (Alternate) 12
10. Chexsystems (Request Report) 14
11. Chexsystems (Request Investigation) 15
12. Request for Loan Modification 16
13. Letter of Hardship for Loan Modification 17
14. Letter of Hardship for Loan Modification (Alternate) 19
15. Letter of Hardship for Loan Modification (Alternate 2) 21
16. Letter to Dismiss Court Judgement 22
17. Request Credit Report 23
18. Dispute Credit Report Items (Round 1) 24
19. Dispute Credit Card Bill 25
20. Error on Credit Card Bill 26
21. Request Removal of Incorrect Info 27
22. Request Removal of Incorrect Info (Alternate) 28
23. Request Direct Negotiation with Creditor 29
24. Pay for Delete (Offer Payment if Negative is Removed) 30
25. Pay for Delete (Alternate) 31
26. Pay for Delete (Alternate 2) 32
27. Debt Settlement Offer 33
28. Debt Settlement Offer (Alternate) 34

29. Debt Settlement Offer (Alternate 2) ... 35
30. Debt Settlement Offer (Alternate 3) ... 36
31. Debt Settlement Offer to Dismiss Court Judgement ... 37
32. Unilateral Release of Claims (Include with Settlement Offer before payment) ... 39
33. Cashed Check Constitutes Payment in Full ... 40
34. Request Smaller Payments (Short Term) ... 43
35. Request Smaller Payments (Long Term) ... 44
36. Request No Payments (Short Term) ... 45
37. Request No Payments (Long Term) ... 46
38. Remove Hard Inquiry ... 47
39. Remove Hard Inquiry (Alternate) ... 48
40. Disputer item ... 49
41. Dispute Item (Alternate) ... 50
42. Validation Of Debt (Simple) ... 51
43. Validation Of Debt (Alternate) ... 52
44. Validation Of Debt (Alternate 2) ... 53
45. Validation Of Debt (Alternate 3) ... 54
46. Validation Of Debt (Alternate 4) ... 56
47. Validation of Debt (After Dispute to Bureau) ... 57
48. Validation of Debt (Estoppel by Silence) ... 58
49. Validation of Debt Request ... 59
50. Validation of Debt (Admission by Silence) ... 60
51. Validation of Debt with Creditor Disclosure Statement ... 62
52. Validation of Debt with Creditor Disclosure Statement (Alternate) ... 64
53. Validation of Debt with Creditor Disclosure Statement (Alternate 2) ... 67
54. Validation of Medical Debt (HIPPAA Request) ... 69
55. Goodwill Letter sent to Original Creditor ... 71
56. Goodwill Adjustment Letter ... 72
57. Inform A Creditor you have filed Bankruptcy ... 73
58. Inform Creditor of Bankruptcy ... 74
59. Agreement Offer Settlement to Dismiss Judgement ... 76

60. Agreement to Dismiss Court Judgement ... 78
61. Judgement Proof Letter ... 79
62. Judgement Proof Letter (Alternate) ... 80
63. Request Original Creditor to Take Back Debt from Collection Agency ... 81
64. Warning of VOD refusal and FDCPA violations ... 82
65. Warning Violation for Expired Debt Collection ... 84
66. Warning Violation for Expired Debt Collection (Alternate) ... 85
67. Warning of Expired Statute of Limitations ... 86
68. Pay For Delete (Alternate 3) ... 87
69. Dispute Credit Report Items (Round 1 Alternate) ... 88
70. Dispute Credit Report Items (Round 1 Alternate 2) ... 89
71. Dispute Credit Report Items Round 1 Alternate 3) ... 90
72. Request Removal after Bureau Investigation ... 91
73. Request Removal after Creditor Verification ... 92
74. Dispute Follow-up after no response for 30 days ... 94
75. Dispute Follow-up after no response for 60 days ... 95
76. Dispute After Investigation: 'The Prove it" Letter ... 96
77. Request to Describe Investigation Procedures ... 97
78. Demand to Comply with Investigation Request ... 98
79. Dispute Accounts That Should Be Included in BK ... 99
80. Validate Debt ... 100
81. Report Identity Theft ... 101
82. Report Identity Theft (Alternate) ... 102
83. Request to Merge Spouse's Credit History ... 104
84. Request to Add Additional Credit Information ... 105
85. Credit Inquiry Removal Request ... 106
86. 100 Word Consumer Statement ... 107
87. Frivolous Dispute Response ... 108
88. Frivolous Dispute Response (Alternate) ... 109
89. Reply to Accusation to Credit Repair ... 110
90. Debt Settlement Offer (Alternate) ... 112

91. Intention to File FTC Complaint – After 30 Days ... 114
92. Intention to File FTC Complaint – After 30 Days (Alternate) ... 115
93. Intention to File FTC Complaint – After 60 Days ... 116
94. Intent to File Lawsuit for FCRA Violation ... 117
95. Dispute Collections ... 118
96. Temporarily Stop Collections ... 120
97. Cease and Desist ... 121
98. Cease and Desist (Alternative) ... 122
99. Cease and Desist (Alternative 2) ... 123
100. Complaint about Harassment ... 124
101. Warning of VOD Refusal and FDCPA Violations ... 125
102. Warning Violation for Expired Debt Collection ... 127
103. Warning Violation for Expired Debt Collection (Alternate) ... 128
104. Warning of Expired Statute of Limitations ... 129

Basic Dispute for Collections

{client_first_name} {client_last_name}
{client_address}
{ss_number}

{creditor_name}
{creditor_address}
{creditor_city}, {creditor_state} {creditor_zip}

{curr_date}

Re: Dispute of Collections Action: Case #{account_number}.

To Whom It May Concern:

I received a copy of my credit report and found the following errors. See the attached copy of my credit report; the errors have been highlighted. Here as follows is error:

{creditor_name}
Account #{account_number}
{dispute_item_and_explanation}

I am hereby requesting that you confirm the fact that I owe this debt as required by any applicable state and federal laws. Please contact the creditor to obtain verification.

In addition, under the provisions of state and federal Fair Debt Collection Practices Act (FDCPA), Fair Credit Reporting Act (FCRA), and related consumer statutes, I am hereby instructing you to cease collection of the debt while efforts are made to obtain verification. Until you resolve this error with the creditor, you should neither contact me nor anyone else except the creditor about this collection.

Furthermore, any reporting of this matter to credit reporting agencies is premature. Until you have investigated my dispute, you should not relay negative information to a credit reporting agency. If negative information has already been reported, you must notify the agency to remove said report until the investigative process is over so that my credit report remains accurate, or at the very least, my credit report should be updated to reflect my dispute.

Your next contact with me should be to either notice that the creditor has failed to provide verification of the debt and that the matter has been closed or that you believe that this debt is valid and are providing proof of my responsibility. If the former, please confirm that I am not being held responsible for the debt in writing and also that if the account has already been noted on my credit report, that you will contact the bureau(s) in question to have the account removed. If the latter, I expect that you will provide me with an explanation as to why you have decided not to remove this account from collections and a copy of all documents relevant to the debt such as the application, bills, records of communications and payments, and any other data that indicates my responsibility.

I am instructing you not to contact any third parties such as my employer, neighbors, friends or family members. In addition, you may not contact me by phone at work or at my home about this collection activity. All future correspondence should be sent to me in writing.

Please acknowledge that you have received this notice within 14 days.

Sincerely,

{client_signature}
_____
{client_first_name} {client_last_name}

Victim of Identity Theft

{client_first_name} {client_last_name}
{client_address}
{bdate}
{ss_number}
{bureau_address}

{curr_date}

Dear Sir/Madam:

I am contacting you about the compromising of my social security number. I am a victim of Identity Theft. I contacted the Federal Trade Commission and filed a complaint # and contacted the police department and obtained a police report # which both are attached. Please block and remove all information from my credit report, and send me an updated copy of my credit report. The following items do not belong to me and is a result of fraud that I did not authorize:

{dispute_item_and_explanation}
Please block and remove all information resulting from Identity Theft pursuant to FCRA 605B (15 U.S.C. & 1681 c-2) which states that these accounts must be removed within 4 Business Days of receipt.

Also, please send an updated copy of my credit report to the above address. According to the act, there shall be no charge for this updated report. I also request that you please send notices of corrections to anyone who received my credit report in the past six months.

Sincerely,

{client_signature}
_____

{client_first_name} {client_last_name}

Basic Dispute for Creditor or Furnisher

{client_first_name} {client_last_name}

{client_address}

{ss_number}

{creditor_name}

{creditor_address}

{creditor_city}, {creditor_state} {creditor_zip}

{curr_date}

Re: Remove Inaccurate Information from my Credit Reports. Account #{account_number}

To Whom It May Concern:

I received a copy of my credit report and found the following item(s) to be errors. See the attached copy of my credit report; the errors have been highlighted. Here as follows are items in error:

{creditor_name}

Account #{account_number}

{dispute_item_and_explanation}

By the provisions of the Fair Credit Reporting Act, I demand that these items be investigated and removed from my report. I understand that under 15 U.S.C. Sec. 1681i(a), you must complete this investigation within 30 days of receipt of this letter.

Thank you for your time and help in this matter.

Sincerely,

{client_signature}

_____

{client_first_name} {client_last_name}

Validate Debt (609 Letter)

{client_first_name} {client_last_name}

{client_address}

{bureau_address}

{curr_date}

To Whom It May Concern,

This letter is a formal complaint that you are reporting inaccurate and incomplete credit information.

According to the Fair Credit Reporting Act, Section 609 (a)(1)(A), you are required by federal law to verify, through the physical verification of the original signed consumer contract, any and all accounts that you post on a credit report. Otherwise anyone paying for your reporting services could fax, mail or email in a fraudulent account.

I demand to see verifiable proof (i.e.: an original consumer contract with my signature on it) that you have on file for the account listed below.

Your failure to positively verify these accounts has hurt my ability to obtain credit. Under the FCRA, unverifiable accounts must be removed and if you are unable to provide me a copy of verifiable proof, you must remove the account listed below.

I demand that the following account be verified or removed immediately:

{dispute_item_and_explanation}

In addition, please remove all non-account holding inquiries over 30 days old. Also, please add a promotional suppression to my credit file.

Under federal law, you have thirty (30) days to complete your re-investigation. Be advised that the description of the procedure used to determine the accuracy and completeness of the information is hereby requested as well, to be provided within fifteen (15) days of the completion of your re-investigation.

Thank you,

{client_signature}

_____

{client_first_name} {client_last_name}

Method of Verification (MOD)

[When the bureau responds to your dispute and request for verification/validation, their response may be vague. For instance, they will sometimes just say "verified" without offering actual proof. When this happens, you have the right by law to challenge how the credit bureau came to the decision. FCRA Act Section 611, gives you the right to request an explanation of the verification method used by the CRA. If either party has the records you can request a copy under the FACTA act, SEC 312 (b) and (c). This document will need modifications depending on the situation. See the notes below (in bold). Add those modifications when you're in the final step of the CRC Dispute Wizard 3 (the final viewer/editor page) and then delete these instructions]

{client_first_name} {client_last_name}

{client_address}

{bdate}

{ss_number}

{bureau_address}

Attn: Customer Relations Department

{curr_date}

Re: Request to describe method of verification

To Whom It May Concern:

I am writing to request the method of verification for dispute initiated on [ENTER DATE HERE] and the subsequent response received on [ENTER CORRECT DATE HERE] enclosed with this letter.

Re: {dispute_item_and_explanation} [Manually modify this line when you're in the final step of the dispute wizard (editor page)]

Please send the following information used to verify the validity of [Manually type in the items you're wanting them to describe, i.e.; identify item(s) by the name of the source, such as creditor or tax court, and the type of item, such as credit account, judgment, etc.]:

The name of the original creditor

The creditors address and telephone number

The person's name they verified the dispute with

The documentation used to verify the disputeIn accordance with FCRA, Section 611, I am requesting this information to review for completeness and accuracy and appropriateness. In lieu of sending the information you can reopen the dispute and ensure a proper investigation is performed.I would appreciate a timely response outlining the steps that will occur to resolve this matter. If I do not receive a response I will have no choice but to exercise my right under FRCA, Section 616, and pursue legal action.

Sincerely,

{client_signature}

{client_first_name} {client_last_name}

Method of Verification (MOD) Alternate

[When the bureau responds to your dispute and request for verification/validation, their response may be vague. For instance, they will sometimes just say "verified" without offering actual proof. When this happens, you have the right by law to challenge how the credit bureau came to the decision. FCRA Act Section 611, gives you the right to request an explanation of the verification method used by the CRA. If either party has the records you can request a copy under the FACTA act, SEC 312 (b) and (c). This document will need modifications depending on the situation. See the notes below (in bold). Add those modifications when you're in the final step of the CRC Dispute Wizard 3 (the final viewer/editor page) and then delete these instructions]

{bureau_address}

Attn: Customer Relations Department

{curr_date}

[TodaysDate]

[RecipientName]

Re: {dispute_item_and_explanation} [Manually modify this line when you're in the final step of the dispute wizard (editor page)]

To Whom It May Concern:

I am concerned about the validity and accuracy of your recent investigation of these accounts that are reporting on my credit report. Last month I requested an investigation because I felt the item was not being reported legally. Couple of days ago I received a letter stating that your investigation was complete. Please explain to me how you conducted your investigation!

1. Please explain to me what your representatives uncovered to lead them to believe that you are reporting this item as it legally should be reported?

2. What certified documents were reviewed to conclude your investigation?

3. Please provide a complete copy of all of the information that was transmitted to the data furnisher as part of the investigation.

4. What did it cost your company to obtain the documents needed to complete your investigation?

5. Please provide proof of your timely procurement of certified documents.

6. Did you speak directly to any agent of the company that was reporting the information to confirm the accuracy of what you are reporting?

7. If yes to above:

   a. Who did you speak to?

   b. On what date?

   c. How long was the conversation?

   d. What was their position?

   e. What telephone number did you call?

f. What is the name of the employee of your company that spoke directly to the above party?

g. What is the position of the employee of your company that spoke directly to the above party?

h. How long has that employee been employed by your company?

i. What formal training was provided to this employee to investigate items of this kind?

j. Was there any e-mail or written communication between members of your company and the above party?

8. If so, please provide copies of all correspondence; supply copies of any and all conclusive documentation to prove that you have in fact conducted a reasonable investigation of the account in question.

9. Provide the date of the commencement of delinquency

10. Provide the SPECIFIC date reporting that these items will cease

Enclosed with your response to the above questions I respectfully request a notarized affidavit confirming the information that is provided is true and correct as per my civil rights granted under several federal laws. This information should not come as a form letter response.

My initial dispute was detailed and directly related to the account in question. A template response will not be an acceptable response. If you cannot supply ALL of the above information in a timely manner as detailed in several laws, including but not limited to the Fair Credit Reporting Act, I must immediately demand the permanent removal of this item from my credit report.

This erroneous entry is detrimental to my overall credit rating and has caused me severe financial and emotional distress. If you choose not to provide the above requested deletion or requested/required documentation of your investigation, I will pursue the enforcements of

my constitutional rights via federal court proceedings. As you are well aware this information will come out through my formal discovery process, and necessary depositions. I have recently studied constitutional consumer protection laws along with civil/federal court procedures. I will represent myself pro-se and will formally request a jury trial.

Please respond accordingly,

{client_signature}

{client_first_name} {client_last_name}

{client_address}

{bdate}

{ss_number}

ChexSystem (Request Report)

***************Instructions delete these before saving and sending**************

Here is a letter for requesting a report from Chexsystems. Chexsystems stores data like a credit bureau for banking and financial institutions and they must follow the same rules as the Credit Bureaus and must maintain the same accuracy when reporting about your checking account history.

***************Instructions delete these before saving and sending**************

{client_first_name} {client_last_name}

{client_address}

{curr_date}

ChexSystems

Attn: Consumer Relations

7805 Hudson Road, Suite 100

Woodbury, MN 55125

By phone at 800-428-9623 or fax at 602-659-2197

To Whom It May Concern,

When I recently tried to open a checking account, I was informed that I had negative entries in my ChexSystems record.

To my knowledge, have never had non-sufficient funds and I am not aware of any negative entries. Kindly forward me a copy of my ChexSystems record so that I may verify its accuracy.

Kind regards,

{client_signature}

_____

{client_first_name} {client_last_name}

ss# {ss_number}

ChexSystems (Request Investigation)

***************Instructions delete these before saving and sending***************

Here is a letter for requesting an investigation from Chexsystems. Chexsystems stores data like a credit bureau for banking and financial institutions and they must follow the same rules as the Credit Bureaus and must maintain the same accuracy when reporting about your checking account history.

***************Instructions delete these before saving and sending***************

{client_first_name} {client_last_name}

{client_address}

{curr_date}

ChexSystems

Attn: Consumer Relations

7805 Hudson Road, Suite 100

Woodbury, MN 55125

To Whom It May Concern,

I received a copy of my ChexSystems record and I have found several inaccuracies in the report.

{dispute_item_and_explanation}

In detail, you recorded that I had non-sufficient funds with [name of bank] on or around [date]. I am disputing this record because I believe it to be inaccurate. Please request evidence of this unresolved outstanding negative record from [bank name] and investigate this item for me.

I understand that your repository is required by law to begin an investigation for me because you are a credit-reporting agency and must follow the Fair Credit Reporting Act. I await your results.

Kind regards,

{client_signature}

_____

{client_first_name} {client_last_name}

ss# {ss_number}

Request for Loan Modification

***************Instructions delete these before saving and sending***************

Instructions: Include Loan Modification Proposal, Hardship Letter, Monthly Expense Worksheet, Monthly Income Worksheet, Schedule of Real Estate Owned, Copy of recent mortgage statement, Copy of any delinquency notices, notice of default, or any other pertinent documents, Past 2 years tax returns, Past 2 months pay stubs, Past 2 months bank statements, Last 6 months profit and loss (if self-employed), Copy of drivers license, 4506T - Form

***************Instructions delete these before saving and sending***************

Loan Modification Request- 1st Mortgage

{client_first_name} {client_last_name}

{client_address}

{t_no}

{creditor_name}

{creditor_address}

{curr_date}

Re: Loan Modification Request- 1st Mortgage Loan # (LOAN NUMBER).

To Whom It May Concern,

Enclosed with this package, you will find my loan modification request and supporting documentation for a loan modification regarding loan number (LOAN NUMBER). After reviewing my income and the current real estate market, you will find that my loan modification request is necessary. In my current situation, the mortgage payments are not

affordable. However, with the proposed loan modification, I will be able to consistently make payments on time and avoid a foreclosure. I would prefer to stay in my home, but if a modification is not possible I will be forced into foreclosure.

Please review the enclosed documents outlining my overall financial situation and real estate market conditions. You may contact me with any questions or requests for further documentation.

Sincerely,

{client_signature}

_____

{client_first_name} {client_last_name}

Letter Of Hardship For Loan Modification

***************Instructions delete these before saving and sending**************

Instructions: Do not copy this letter exactly as written. We suggest that you modify this to letter be unique to your situation and hardship.

***************Instructions delete these before saving and sending**************

{client_first_name} {client_last_name}

{client_address}

{t_no}

{creditor_name}

{creditor_address}

{curr_date}

Re: Letter of Hardship

To Whom It May Concern,

I/We are requesting that Lender, Servicer, PMI, Governmental guarantor or insurer, representing lawyer, or other party related to this case review my financial situation to see if I/We qualify for any workout option.

I/We are having problems making my monthly payments because of financial difficulties created by:

(Unemployment, Reduced Income, Divorce, Medical Bills, Too Much Debt, Death of my Spouse, Payment Increase, Business Failure, Job Relocation, Illness, Military Service, Incarceration or Other -- Please Specify)

I/We believe that my/our situation is (Choose: Temporary / Permanent)

I have recently received a significant pay cut due to the current devastating economy. I used almost all of my savings and it is getting more and more difficult to stay up to date on my mortgage payment. As a result of the outlay in expenses and the bleeding dry of my money, I am struggling to make my mortgage payments. Kindly consider my current situation and consider my request for a short sale. I had every intention on making good on this loan, but at this time it does not like possible.

When I received this mortgage, my mortgage broker promised me a low fixed rate mortgage. When I arrived for the closing, my rate was relatively low; however, it was only fixed for a short time. At the closing table, my broker told me the lender would refinance me in before the loan would reset and pressured me into signing the loan documents. At this time, my rate has gone way up and I cannot get a refinance. There is no equity in my home and the value has dropped tremendously. Please consider us for a short sale, as we see no other option make our housing payments affordable.

Thank you for your assistance and cooperation.

I/We, state the information provided above to be true and correct to the best of my/our knowledge.

Sincerely,

{client_signature}

_____

{client_first_name} {client_last_name}

Letter Of Hardship For Loan Modification (Alternate)

**************Instructions delete these before saving and sending**************

Instructions: Do not copy this letter exactly as written. We suggest that you modify this to letter be unique to your situation and hardship.

**************Instructions delete these before saving and sending**************

{client_first_name} {client_last_name}

{client_address}

{t_no}

{creditor_name}

{creditor_address}

{curr_date}

Re: Letter of Hardship

Borrower: {client_first_name} {client_last_name}

Subject Property: (PROPERTY ADDRESS), Loan Number: ##########

To Whom It May Concern,

I am writing this letter to explain our family's unfortunate situation that has caused us to become delinquent on our mortgage. We have tried everything in our power to keep current on our payments but unfortunately since our interest rate adjusted, we have fallen behind and would like you to consider working with us to reduce our monthly payments.

The main reasons that caused us to become late are a decrease in our income, increase in our monthly obligations, current market conditions, our adjustable rate mortgage, and our inability to refinance.

I work as a waitress and my husband works at a marketing manager for a local screen printing company. Most of my income has been generated by tips and has decreased dramatically due to the unfortunate economic situation. My husband job is secure and he has been with the same company for 2 years. We have a 3 year old son and cannot afford daycare in order to get a second job.

For the past several months we have been cutting back on our misc. expenses. We no longer have premium cable, go on vacations, or eat out. Our credit cards are getting maxed out due to us paying our mortgage on them and can no longer keep that up. We have currently missed 2 payments and wish to work out a payment plan with you after you reduce our rates to something we can afford.

My husband and I consulted mortgage professionals regarding a refinance but due to our lack of equity, the falling home prices in our community, and our lack of assets we were denied.

I have no other choice but to ask you to please consider my request for a loan modification. My family and I would really be grateful if you can help us work out a payment schedule we could afford. We do not want to lose our home. We wish to continue making mortgage payments on time for the remainder of our loan.

Sincerely,

{client_signature}

_____

{client_first_name} {client_last_name}

Letter Of Hardship For Loan Modification (Alternate 2)

***************Instructions delete these before saving and sending***************

Instructions: Do not copy this letter exactly as written. We suggest that you modify this to letter be unique to your situation and hardship.

***************Instructions delete these before saving and sending***************

{client_first_name} {client_last_name}

{client_address}

{t_no}

{creditor_name}

{creditor_address}

{curr_date}

Re: Letter of Hardship

Borrower: {client_first_name} {client_last_name}

Subject Property: (PROPERTY ADDRESS), Loan Number: ##########

To Whom It May Concern:

We are writing to you to explain our current financial situation that has caused us to default on our loan agreement. We don't want to lose our home and will anything we can to work with you to remedy the situation and find a solution that will benefit us both. We first became delinquent on our mortgage payments due to [INSERT YOUR REASON HERE BRIEFLY]. We've tried to bring the account current, but haven't been able to catch up by paying the full amount due. The trouble started approximately [INSERT DATE HERE] and we believe that this is a [TEMPORARY or PERMANENT] hardship.

We are now in a better position and would like to work out a plan to begin making payments again and stay in our home. We are hard working, responsible individuals willing to work to keep our home. We would appreciate it if you would consider a modification to our existing loan terms in order to lower the monthly payment and include some or all of the past due amount. We've created and implemented a new budget for our family and we are confident that we would be able to meet the new, lower monthly payment every month without fail. We'd appreciate any help or suggestions you could give to us regarding this matter. It's an extremely difficult time for our family and we'd really like to get the issue resolved as soon as possible.

Sincerely,

{client_signature}

_____

{client_first_name} {client_last_name}

Letter to Dismiss Court Judgment

{client_first_name} {client_last_name}

{client_address}

[Creditor/Furnisher]

[Creditor/Furnisher Address]

Re: Agreement to Dismiss Court Judgment

Court Name and Location: (COURT NAME AND LOCATION)

Judgment Creditor: (CREDITOR NAME)

Judgment Debtor: (DEBTOR NAME)

Case Number: (CASE NUMBER)

Judgment: (JUDGMENT # AND INFO)

Date of Entry: (DATE)

We, the undersigned Judgment Creditor and Judgment Debtor have agreed to settle this matter and hereby jointly apply to the court for an order that the judgment involved (enter court case number and date entered) be set aside and dismissed.

_____   _____

Signed: Judgment Credit: Date signed

_____   _____

Judgment Debtor: Date signed

Request Credit Report

{client_first_name} {client_last_name}

{client_address}

Annual Credit Report Request Service

P.O. Box 105281

Atlanta, GA 30348-5281

{curr_date}

Re: Request for Complimentary Annual Credit Reports

To Whom It May Concern,

I am writing to request my complimentary annual credit report from: Experian,

Full Name: {client_first_name} {client_last_name}

{bdate}

{ss_number}

Address: {client_address}

{t_no}

Enclosed are copies of documents identifying me by my name and address.

Thank you for your time and help in this matter.

Sincerely yours,

{client_signature}

_____

{client_first_name} {client_last_name}

Dispute Credit Report Items (Round 1)

{client_first_name} {client_last_name}

{client_address}

{t_no}

{bdate}

{ss_number}

{bureau_address}

{curr_date}

Re: Letter to Remove Inaccurate Credit Information: Report # {report_number}

To Whom It May Concern:

I received a copy of my credit report and found the following item(s) to be in error:

{dispute_item_and_explanation}

By the provisions of the Fair Credit Reporting Act, I demand that these items be investigated and removed from my report. It is my understanding that you will recheck these items with the creditor who has posted them. Please remove any information that the creditor cannot verify. I understand that under 15 U.S.C. Sec. 1681i(a), you must complete this reinvestigation within 30 days of receipt of this letter.

Please send an updated copy of my credit report to the above address. According to the act, there shall be no charge for this updated report. I also request that you please send notices of corrections to anyone who received my credit report in the past six months.

Thank you for your time and help in this matter.

Sincerely,

{client_signature}

_____

{client_first_name} {client_last_name}

Dispute Credit Card Bill

{client_first_name} {client_last_name}

{client_address}

{creditor_name}

{creditor_email}

{creditor_city} {creditor_state} {creditor_zip}

{curr_date}

Re: Account number: {client_ac_no}

To Whom It May Concern:

I am writing to dispute the following charge(s) that appear on my billing statement dated (STATEMENT DATE):

(MERCHANT'S NAME)

(AMOUNT IN ERROR)

The error is as follows:

(REASON FOR COMPLAINT)

As required by law, I have tried in good faith to resolve this dispute with the merchant:

(ENTER STEPS TAKEN)

Furthermore, I wish to point out that this purchase was for more than $50 and was made (CHOOSE ONE:) in the state in which I live [OR] within 100 miles of my home.

Please verify this dispute with the merchant and remove this item, and all late and interest charges associated with this item, from my billing statement.

Thank you for your time and assistance.

Sincerely yours,

{client_signature}

_____

{client_first_name} {client_last_name}

Error on Credit Card Bill

{client_first_name} {client_last_name}

{client_address}

{creditor_name}

{creditor_address}

{creditor_city}, {creditor_state} {creditor_zip}

{curr_date}

Re: Account number: {account_number}

To Whom It May Concern:

I am writing to report an error I have discovered on my billing statement

dated (STATEMENT DATE):

(MERCHANT'S NAME)

(AMOUNT IN ERROR)

The error is as follows:

(REASON FOR COMPLAINT)

I understand that the law requires you to acknowledge receipt of this letter within 30 days unless you correct this billing error before then. Furthermore, I understand that within two billing cycles (but in no event more than 90 days), you must correct the error or explain why you believe the amount to be correct.

Thank you for your time and assistance.

Sincerely yours,

{client_signature}

{client_first_name} {client_last_name}

Request Removal of Incorrect Info

{client_first_name} {client_last_name}

{client_address}

{creditor_name}

{creditor_address}

{creditor_city}, {creditor_state} {creditor_zip}

{curr_date}

{client_first_name} {client_last_name}, Account number: {account_number}

To Whom It May Concern:

On (DATE), I received a copy of my credit history report from (CREDIT BUREAU NAME). That Report contained incorrect information reported by you.

I contacted the (CREDIT BUREAU NAME) to request deletion of this inaccurate data from my Credit History Report, but they have refused. They insist that your company claims this information to be accurately reported. This is not true, and here as follows is the correct information:

{dispute_item_and_explanation}

I am enclosing the following documentation to support my claim that the information you have reported is not correct:

(LIST DOCUMENTATION)

This negative mark is damaging to my credit. Please contract Experian, Equifax and Trans-Union, immediately to remove this information from my credit file.

Please confirm to me within 20 days that you have contacted the credit bureaus to correct this information.

Thank you for your time and assistance.

Sincerely yours,

{client_signature}

_____

{client_first_name} {client_last_name}

Request Removal of Incorrect Info (Alternate)

{client_first_name} {client_last_name}

{client_address}

{creditor_address}

{curr_date}

To Whom It May Concern,

I have recently received a copy of my credit report. The report had an account listed from your company as a credit card. I disputed the account with the credit bureau as "not mine" but it recently came back as verified.

{dispute_item_and_explanation}

I am writing this letter to you in an effort to get this removed. Please delete your information from my credit reports. I have never had an account with your company. If someone has opened an account in my name, please close it immediately before further harm is done.

I am requesting that you notify all of credit bureaus that this account is "disputed" or that you delete this account until this matter is resolved. This is required by the Fair Credit Reporting Act. If there is any paperwork that I need to sign to confirm that this account is not mine, please send me the required documents.

This is a written dispute of the this account per the Fair Credit Reporting Act, the Fair Debt Collection Practices Act and the Fair Credit Billing Act. Please be aware that I am exercising all of my rights per these laws and all other applicable laws protecting me.

Sincerely,

{client_signature}

_____

{client_first_name} {client_last_name}

Request Direct Negotiation with Creditor

{client_first_name} {client_last_name}

{client_address}

{creditor_name}

{creditor_address}

{creditor_city}, {creditor_state} {creditor_zip}

{curr_date}

Re: {client_first_name} {client_last_name}, Account number: {account_number}

To Whom It May Concern:

I have been contacted several times by {creditor_name} regarding a past due account with you. I do not, however, wish to discuss this matter with them and I have asked them to cease contact with me.

I would prefer to speak directly with the {creditor_name} collections department.

Please pass this information to your collections department and indicate my desire to be in touch with them.

Thank you for your help.

Sincerely yours,

_{client_signature}

_____

{client_first_name} {client_last_name}

Pay for Delete (Offer Payment if Negative is Removed)

{client_first_name} {client_last_name}

{client_address}

{creditor_name}

{creditor_address}

{creditor_city}, {creditor_state} {creditor_zip}

{curr_date}

Re: {client_first_name} {client_last_name} , Account number {account_number}

To Whom It May Concern:

On (Date), I received a copy of my credit report from (Credit Bureau Name). That report lists my payments to you as being 'delinquent.'

My financial problems are now behind me and I am in a position to pay off this debt. I can pay a lump sum amount of $_____ or I can pay installments in the amount of $_____ per month for _____ months if you will agree to one of the following:

( ) If I make a lump sum payment, you will agree to remove all negative information from my credit file associated with the debt.

( ) If I agree to pay off the debt in monthly installments, you agree to 're-age' my account - making the current month the first repayment month and showing no late payments as long as I make the agreed upon monthly payments.

If this offer is acceptable to you, please check and initial one of the above choices, sign your acceptance below and return this letter to me in the enclosed envelope.

Thank you for your time and assistance.

Sincerely yours,

{client_signature}

_____

{client_first_name} {client_last_name}

Agreed to and accepted to on this _____ day of _____, _____.

By: _____

(Creditor Representative Signature)

Name (print): _____

Company: _____

Title: _____

Pay For Delete (Alternate)

{client_first_name} {client_last_name}

{client_address}

{client_previous_address}

{creditor_name}

{creditor_address}

{creditor_city} {creditor_state} {creditor_zip}

{creditor_phone}

{curr_date}

To Whom It May Concern,

Re: {account_number}

This letter is an offer to amicably settle the above account. It shall not be misconstrued as an acknowledgment of any liability for this debt in any form.

I will pay your company the amount of $XXXX as "full settlement of this account.

If you accept this agreement, I will send you a money order or certified cashiers check for this settlement amount of $XXXX in exchange for a full deletion of all references regarding this account from my credit reports and full satisfaction of the debt. This agreement is binding and will be void should you not fulfill your end of this agreement. Furthermore, this debt will be deleted from my credit report at all three credit bureaus, as well as any other bureaus that your company regularly reports to.

If you agree to the above, please acknowledge with your signature and return a copy to me. Upon receipt of your signed acknowledgment, I will promptly send you a money order or cashiers check in the amount I have stated above.

Please note: This agreement is restricted. This is not a renewed promise to pay, but rather a restricted settlement offer only. By not signing below, you agree that the debt has not been renewed nor have any written agreements been exchanged.

I look forward to resolving this matter in a speedily manner.

{client_first_name} {client_last_name}

Creditor's Authorized Signature: _____

Date:_____

Name: _____

Title : _____

Pay For Delete (Alternate 2)

{client_first_name} {client_last_name}

{client_address}

{client_previous_address}

{creditor_name}

{creditor_address}

{creditor_city} {creditor_state} {creditor_zip}

{creditor_phone}

{curr_date}

Dear Collection Manager:

It has come to my attention, through my credit report, that you claim I owe a debt to your agency. I can save us both some effort and time by settling the debt out.Here below is my offer. This is not a renewed promise to pay, nor does it constitute any agreement unless you sign and return it. Please Note that I have not yet agreed that this debt is indeed mine and I have the option to seek additional proof of this debt from your agency.Because you hold all the rights to report the debt to the credit bureaus as you see fit, you can certainly change that listing at any time as the source reporting the debt.I have no doubt that you are aware of my right to dispute this debt and request full proof of obligation. Paying this unverified debt to you has little value to me if we cannot mutually agree that you will report the debt as outlined below.While I realize that your function is to collect debts as a collection agent, I am also aware that a paid collection would not be favorable on my report. That being said, I have determined, through the bureaus, that you have the absolute right to report this debt as you see fit or not report it at all.If you indicate that you are unable to remove the negative listing on my credit report, I will be forced to cease communication and request full verification of the debt.My goal is to arrange a term that is acceptable to us both, since this debt is "questionable."My Offer: I will pay your company the amount of $xx as "payment in full for the full satisfaction of this account." Upon receipt of the above payment, your company will agree to change this entry on my credit reports to "Paid" immediately. You further agree to remove any and all previous notations of delinquency.If you approve and agree to these terms, please acknowledge with your signature and return this letter to me. You agree these terms herein are confidential and that you have the authority to make such decisions. No payment will be made without written confirmation.Upon receipt of this signed acknowledgment, I will immediately mail you funds by priority mail. This is not a renewed promise to pay but rather a restricted offer only. If no terms can be met, no new arrangements will be made, and the offer will be withdrawn.

{client_first_name} {client_last_name}

{creditor_name}_____

Signature of company office_____

Print Company Officer name

Sincerely,

Name

Address

Social security number

Debt Settlement Offer

***************Instructions Delete these before saving and sending***************

This is the only way to settle a debt with a collection agency. If they agree to delete. If you have effectively agreed with a creditor or collector to settle a debt, this letter will to secure your rights for amount to be paid and credit reporting issues. Do not use this letter if the debt is disputed or expired, as doing so can renew the statute of limitations. If you agree that the debt is valid and you wish to begin negotiations you may also use this letter to present your first offer.

***************Instructions Delete these before saving and sending***************

{client_first_name} {client_last_name}

{client_address}

{creditor_name}

{creditor_address}

{creditor_city}, {creditor_state} {creditor_zip}

{curr_date}

Re: Debtor's Settlement

Re: Account number: {account_number}

To Whom It May Concern:

I understand that I owe a balance to your company. This letter is an offer to settle the debt for less because of my inability to pay the entire balance. Because of dire financial circumstances, [overwhelming debt, loss of job, insurance settlement with limited funds, considering bankruptcy, borrowing the money, illness, loss of family member with income, etc. List your reason here as to why you are offering to pay less.] I am only able to pay a portion of this debt. I recognize you may be motivated as well, because of the age of the debt and my financial crisis. Declining to work with me will only make matters worse for both of us. You are claiming the amount owed on the account is $_____. Please accept my good faith offer to settle this account under these following conditions ONLY.

The parties involved agree to settle the account in full for the sum of $_____ and this amount is accepted as complete and final payment on said debt. Full discharge and settlement of all monies due will be created, provided that the amount agreed upon shall be paid as follows: Payment terms: how debt will be paid, (i.e., three payments of $250.00 to be paid monthly on the 1st of each month, 8 payments of $200.00 on the 1st of each month after execution of this agreement, etc.)

Payment address: where you will send payment each month.

Other terms: list specific arrangements made, such as, creditor agrees to freeze the account without any additional fees or interest added to the balance etc.

Credit reporting: list all account status terms you are requesting such as "paid in full", "deleted", "settled in full", "settled for less", etc.

Governing states: This agreement shall be binding under the laws of [list your state and the creditor's state].

If your office is in agreement with this settlement, please reply with confirmation on your company letterhead and signed by an individual with the authority to accept such offers. Time is of the essence because of my financial situation so please reply as soon as possible.

Kind regards, _____

{client_first_name} {client_last_name}

Debt Settlement Offer (Alternate)

{client_first_name} {client_last_name}

{client_address}

{creditor_name}

{creditor_address}

{creditor_city} {creditor_state} {creditor_zip}

{curr_date}

Re: Debtor's Settlement Offer for Account Number: {account_number}

To Whom It May Concern,

I am aware that I owe a balance to your company. This letter is an offer to settle the debt for less because of my inability to pay the full balance due to financial circumstances, because of: (LIST HARDSHIPS HERE), I am only able to pay a portion of this debt.

I realize you may be motivated as well, because of the age of the debt and my financial crisis. Refusing to work with me will only make matters worse for both of us.

You claim the amount owed on the account is $_____.

Please accept this offer to settle this account ONLY under the following conditions:

The parties involved agree to settle the account in full for the sum of $_____ and this amount is accepted as full and final payment on said debt. Complete discharge and settlement of all monies due will be created, provided that the amount agreed upon shall be paid in the following manner:

Payment terms: (i.e., 10 payments of $XXX on the 1st of each month after the execution of this agreement, 3 payments of $XXX to be paid monthly on the 1st of each month, 1 lump sum of $XXXX, etc.)

Payment location: (ADDRESS TO SEND THE PAYMENTS

Other terms: (list additional arrangements made, such as, creditor agrees to freeze the account without any additional fees or interest added to the balance, etc.) Credit reporting: (list status terms you are requesting such as "paid in full", "settled in full", "Paid as agreed", "settled for less", "deleted" etc.)

This agreement shall be binding under the laws of (LIST YOUR STATE AND THE CREDITOR'S STATE)If your office agrees to this settlement, please send back confirmation on your company letterhead and signed by someone with the authority to accept such offers. Time is of the essence due to my present financial situation so please reply as soon as possible.

Sincerely,

{client_signature}

_____

{client_first_name} {client_last_name}

Debt Settlement Offer (Alternate 2)

**********************Instructions - Delete Before Printing**************************

Send this only if the Creditor or Collections Agent has already agreed by phone or correspondence.

**********************Instructions - Delete Before Printing**************************

{client_first_name} {client_last_name}

{client_address}

{creditor_name}

{creditor_address}

{creditor_city} {creditor_state} {creditor_zip}

Attn: Attn: Settlement Dept.

{curr_date}

Re: Debtor's Settlement Offer for Account Number: {account_number}

Dear Settlement Dept.:

This is a settlement offer for {client_first_name} {client_last_name}, (Debtor) concerning a debt owed to (Creditor), who claims the amount to be owed on Account Number:

{account_number} is $(AMOUNT).

Please accept this offer to settle this account under the following conditions:

The parties agree to settle the account in full for the sum of $(AMOUNT) and this amount is accepted as full and total payment on said debt provided the following is met. {client_first_name} {client_last_name} will pay cashiers check of $(AMOUNT) if the debt is considered paid in full and reported as such to the credit reporting agencies. The creditor agrees to freeze the account without any additional fees or interest being added to the balance, provided debtor fulfills the agreed upon settlement obligations. The account is marked: (list status terms you are requesting such as "paid in full", "settled in full", "Paid as agreed", "settled for less", "deleted" etc.) This agreement shall be governed under the laws of (STATE), and shall be binding. If the above terms are acceptable to (CREDITOR), please respond in writing, on your company letterhead, acknowledging your acceptance and the terms as you agree to them. As soon as I receive your acceptance of this offer, I will express mail a cashiers' check.

_____

Creditor name   _____   Creditor: Title:

I agree to the terms listed above: Yes____ No____

_____Creditor's Authorized Signature   Date

Debt Settlement Offer (Alternate 3)

*************************Instructions - Delete Before Printing*************************

Send this only if the Creditor or Collections Agent has already agreed by phone or correspondance.

*************************Instructions - Delete Before Printing*************************

{client_first_name} {client_last_name}

{client_address}

{creditor_name}

{creditor_address}

{creditor_city} {creditor_state} {creditor_zip}

Re: Account Number: {account_number}.

Dear {creditor_name},

This is to confirm our conversation on _____ as to the offer of the above stated account. As discussed, I will pay your company the amount of $_____ as payment in full for the final satisfaction of this account. Upon receipt of the above payment, your company has agreed to change the entry on my credit reports from: _____ to (list status terms you are requesting, such as "paid in full", "settled in full", "Paid as agreed", "settled for less", "deleted" etc.) . If you agree with these terms, please acknowledge with your signature and return it to me. You agree the terms herein are confidential and you have the authority to make such decisions. No payment will be made without written confirmation. Upon receipt of this signed acknowledgment, I will immediately mail you funds priority mail. This is not a renewed promise to pay but rather a restricted offer only. If no terms can be met, no new arrangements will be made and the offer will be void.

_____

Name of Creditor

_____

Creditor's Authorized Signature   Date

_____

Name Of Creditor's Authorized Representative

_____

Position or Title:

Debt Settlement Offer to Dismiss Court Judgment

{client_first_name} {client_last_name}

{client_address}

{creditor_name}

{creditor_address}

To: Judgment Creditor, {creditor_name}

From: Judgment Debtor, {client_first_name} {client_last_name}

Case number: (CASE NUMBER)

Judgment amount: (AMOUNT)

Date: {curr_date}

Dear Sir,

I am aware of the money due you and of the judgment placed against me for this money. I had every intention of taking care of this prior to the entry of the judgment, but unfortunately time constraints ended that chance.

Today I am writing to you so that we may put this matter behind us and settle out this judgment for good, under a few conditions. This will save you time and money trying to collect the judgment and will help me recover from your negative entry against me.

I have been offered an amount from a close family member to pay you $(AMOUNT) to settle the debt in full and have the judgment dismissed.

As the judgment creditor, you reserve the right to dismiss or vacate the judgment as well as entering it. If I pay you from this offer letter saving you immense time, fees and paperwork, you can then file a simple paper with the courts dismissing the judgment.

My offer is to pay you in exchange for the dismissal so that we have both gained something from this unfortunate situation. It is extremely important that you dismiss the judgment rather than satisfying it, because a satisfied judgment really looks no better for me than a filed judgment.

With a dismissed judgment I can justify paying you. Upon your signed approval of this offer, I will forward the full settlement to you immediately. I understand this offer is void if I do not send you $(AMOUNT) within 5-10 days of your signed confirmation.

If you agree to "dismiss" the judgment upon full and final payment of $(AMOUNT), then please sign and return this offer and acceptance.

Offer Accepted and Agreed,

_____

Judgment Creditor Signature   Date

_____

Judgment Creditor Authorized Representative

On behalf of:

_____

Judgment Creditor Company Name

Unilateral Release of Claims (Include with Settlement Offer Before Payment)

{client_first_name} {client_last_name}

{client_address}

{creditor_name}

{creditor_address}

{creditor_city} {creditor_state} {creditor_zip}

Re: Account Number: {account_number}. Balance to be paid: $_____

Dear {creditor_name}

Per our agreement to settle the above mentioned debt, I am requesting that you sign this unilateral release form. This form confirms that we both agreed to settle the debt listed above for the amount indicated.

Creditors/Agency Name: _____

We agree that to accept $_____ as "payment in full" for account number: {account_number}.

For: {client_first_name} {client_last_name}

We will accept this amount as full and final satisfaction and we will have no future claims against this account or debtor. This Unilateral Release ensures that we understand we have accepted a settlement on this debt and will not pursue the debtor later for any deficiency balance.

_____

Creditor's Authorized Signature   Date

_____

Printed name of Creditors Authorized Rep.

_____

Position or Title:

Cashed Check Constitutes Payment in Full

(*NOTE: THIS LETTER IS IN TWO PARTS. DELETE THE SECTIONS THAT YOU DO NOT NEED)

{client_first_name} {client_last_name}

{client_address}

{creditor_name}

{creditor_address}

{creditor_city}, {creditor_state} {creditor_zip}

{curr_date}

Re: {client_first_name} {client_last_name} , Account number: {account_number}

To Whom It May Concern:

This letter concerns the money I owe you. I have received bills from you stating that I owe (AMOUNT OF BILL). However, I am disputing the amount owed to you because of the following reasons:

(LIST REASONS FOR DISPUTE)

I feel I owe you no more than $(ENTER AMOUNT). It is obvious that there is a good faith dispute over this bill.

To settle this debt, I will send you a check for $(ENTER AMOUNT) with a restrictive endorsement; if you cash that check it will constitute an accord and satisfaction. In other words; you will receive from me a check that states "cashing of this check constitutes payment in full." If you cash this check, that check will clear away any debt that I owe you.

If agreed, please sign and return this letter.

Thank you for your time and assistance.

Sincerely yours,

{client_signature}

_____

{client_first_name} {client_last_name}

Agreed to and accepted to on this _____ day of _____, _____.

By:

_____

(Creditor Representative's Signature)

Name (print):_____

Title (print):_____

Company (print):_____

LETTER 2 (OF 2) TO BE SENT WITH YOUR CHECK (AFTER 30 DAYS):**

{client_first_name} {client_last_name}

{client_address}

{creditor_name}

{creditor_address}

{creditor_city}, {creditor_state}, {creditor_zip}

{curr_date}

Re: Account number: {account_number}

To Whom It May Concern:

Enclosed is a check for $(Amount) to cover the balance of Account Number: {account_number}.

This check is tendered in accordance with my letter dated (Date of First Letter). If you cash this check, you agree that my debt has been paid off in full.

Sincerely yours,

{client_signature}

_____

{client_first_name} {client_last_name}

(**Important: Write on the bottom of the check on the front along the top or bottom the exact language you used in the second letter"This check is tendered in accordance with my letter of (DATE OF FIRST LETTER). If you cash this check you agree that my debt is paid in full.")

Request Smaller Payments (Short Term)

{client_first_name} {client_last_name}

{client_address}

{creditor_name}

{creditor_address}

{creditor_city}, {creditor_state} {creditor_zip}

{curr_date}

Re: Account number: {account_number}, Request for Reduced Payments

To Whom It May Concern:

In my current financial situation, I am unable to pay the required monthly payments as originally agreed. My financial position is described below:

(STATE REASON)

I am able to pay $_____ per month starting on _____, and I expect to resume making the full monthly payment on or before _____.

It would help me so much if you would accept this reduced payment schedule. If necessary, you may add the unpaid amount to the end of the account period and extend it by the appropriate number of months.

Thank you for your consideration and understanding. Please let me know within 20 days if the foregoing proposal is acceptable.

Sincerely yours,

{client_signature}

_____

{client_first_name} {client_last_name}

Request Smaller Payments (Long Term)

{client_first_name} {client_last_name}

{client_address}

{creditor_name}

{creditor_address}

{creditor_city}, {creditor_state} {creditor_zip}

{curr_date}

Re: Account number: {account_number}, Request for Reduced Payments

To Whom It May Concern:

In my current financial situation, I am unable to pay the required monthly payments as originally agreed. My financial position is described below:

(STATE REASON)

I am able to pay $_____ per month starting on _____, and I expect to resume making the full monthly payment on or before _____.

It would help me so much if you would accept this reduced payment schedule. If necessary, you may add the unpaid amount to the end of the account period and extend it by the appropriate number of months.

Thank you for your consideration and understanding. Please let me know within 20 days if the foregoing proposal is acceptable.

Sincerely yours,

{client_signature}

_____

{client_first_name} {client_last_name}

Request No Payments (Short Term)

{client_first_name} {client_last_name}

{client_address}

{creditor_name}

{creditor_address}

{creditor_city}, {creditor_state} {creditor_zip}

{curr_date}

Re: Account number: {account_number}, Request for Reduced Payments

To Whom It May Concern:

In my current financial situation, I am unable to pay the required monthly payments as originally agreed. My financial position is described below:

(STATE REASON)

At the present time, I cannot make any payments. I expect to resume making the full monthly payment when the following occurs:

(STATE REASON)

If necessary, you may add the unpaid amount to the end of the account period and extend it by the appropriate number of months.

Thank you for your consideration and understanding. Please let me know within 20 days if the foregoing proposal is acceptable.

Sincerely yours,

{client_signature}

_____

{client_first_name} {client_last_name}

Request No Payments (Long Term)

{client_first_name} {client_last_name}

{client_address}

{creditor_name}

(CREDITOR Address)

{creditor_city}, {creditor_state} {creditor_zip}

{curr_date}

Name(s) on account: {client_first_name} {client_last_name}

Account number: {account_number}

Re: Request for Reduced Payments

To Whom It May Concern:

In my current financial situation, I am unable to pay the required monthly payments as originally agreed. My financial position is described below:

(STATE REASON)

Due to my desperate financial situation, I cannot make any payments for the indefinite future.

(DESCRIBE YOUR HARDSHIP)

I promise to inform you immediately should my financial condition improve and I am able to resume sending you normal payments.

Thank you for your consideration and understanding. Please let me know within 20 days if the foregoing proposal is acceptable.

Sincerely yours,

{client_signature}

_____

{client_first_name} {client_last_name}

Remove Hard Inquiry

{client_first_name} {client_last_name}

{client_address}

{creditor_name}

{creditor_address}

{creditor_city}, {creditor_state} {creditor_zip}

{curr_date}

To Whom it May Concern

According to my most recent credit report, your company is currently reporting to the three credit bureaus that I applied for credit with your organization. I did not grant you authorization to review my credit report

The Fair Credit Reporting Act requires that a creditor be able to verify the written authorization of the consumer giving the creditor permission to review their credit. If you can provide a copy of a credit application authorizing the disclosure of my credit files with my signature, I will accept the inquiry. If a signed authorization cannot be found please remove the inquiry from the three main credit bureaus

The presence of this inquiry is adversely affecting my credit report and is impeding my ability to obtain necessary credit. Time is of the essence so I would greatly appreciate a response from you within thirty (30) days

Please mail me the copy of the signed application or a letter indicating your intention to delete the inquiry.

Sincerely yours,

{client_signature}

_____

{client_first_name} {client_last_name}

Remove Hard Inquiry (Alternate)

{client_address}

{creditor_name}

{creditor_address}

{creditor_city} {creditor_state} {creditor_zip}

{curr_date}

Re: Unauthorized Credit Inquiry

To Whom It May Concern,

I received a copy of my credit report today and discovered a hard inquiry from your company. I do not recall authorizing this inquiry and I would like to see the application of credit. Under the Fair Credit Reporting Act, no one may access my credit without my permission for the purpose of extending credit.

I am sending this letter certified mail for my protection as well as yours. Please forward proof to me at your earliest convenience or send a request to the credit bureaus that you report to if you discover this was an error.

It is urgent that I hear from you urgently, as this hard inquiry is impacting my credit score.

I anticipate your response.

Sincerely,

{client_signature}

_____

{client_first_name} {client_last_name}

Dispute Item

{client_first_name} {client_last_name}

{client_address}

{creditor_name}

{creditor_address}

{creditor_city}, {creditor_state} {creditor_zip}

{curr_date}

To Whom It May Concern,

Your company is currently reporting a negative listing to the three major credit bureaus (Experian, Trans Union, and Equifax) regarding the above referenced account. Based on my recollection and my records, I can find no reason for you reporting such a history. If you'll review your records I think that you will find your reported notations are inaccurate.

The erroneous status of your credit reporting agency records is unacceptable and is preventing me from obtaining necessary financing. Pursuant to Title 15, Section 1666 of the United States Code, I formally request the following documentary evidence pertaining to my account:

A summary of all account activities, including all payments made, late charges, interest, date of payments received, date of payments posted, charges made and date of charges posted.

Copies of all documents and financial instruments used to pay the disputed late payments.

Copies of all charge slips, invoices, promissory notes, and all other documents proving indebtedness.

This information and documentation is critical and time is of the essence. Within less than thirty (30) days, I will be damaged partially because of the discrepancy with your reported records. The above noted code requires your response within thirty (30) days. Your prompt attention will be greatly appreciated. I hereby request that your response be mailed to the address listed below.

If you find that your information and documentation does not support the negative history reported to the three credit bureaus, I invite you to submit a completed Universal Data Form to said bureaus in order to remove the negative notations. Upon removal of the negative notations, I agree to hold your company harmless from any and all inconvenience and/or damage related thereto.

Sincerely,

{client_signature}

_____

{client_first_name} {client_last_name}

Dispute Item (Alternate)

{client_first_name} {client_last_name}

{client_address}

{creditor_address}

{curr_date}

To Whom It May Concern,

I have recently received a copy of my credit report. The report had an account listed from your company as a credit card. I disputed the account with the credit bureau as "not mine" but it recently came back as verified.

{dispute_item_and_explanation}

I am writing this letter to you in an effort to get this removed. Please delete your information from my credit reports. I have never had an account with your company. If someone has opened an account in my name, please close it immediately before further harm is done.

I am requesting that you notify all of credit bureaus that this account is "disputed" or that you delete this account until this matter is resolved. This is required by the Fair Credit Reporting Act. If there is any paperwork that I need to sign to confirm that this account is not mine, please send me the required documents.

This is a written dispute of the this account per the Fair Credit Reporting Act, the Fair Debt Collection Practices Act and the Fair Credit Billing Act. Please be aware that I am exercising all of my rights per these laws and all other applicable laws protecting me.

Sincerely,

{client_signature}

_____

{client_first_name} {client_last_name}

Validation of Debt (Simple)

{client_first_name} {client_last_name}

{client_address}

{creditor_name}

{creditor_address}

{creditor_city} {creditor_state} {creditor_zip}

{curr_date}

Re: Account # {account_number}

To Whom It May Concern,

I dispute your claims in their entirety and I am requesting validation from you pursuant to the Fair Debt Collection Practices Act, 15 USC 1692g Sec. 809 (8) (FDCPA).

Sincerely,

{client_signature}

_____

{client_first_name} {client_last_name}

Validation of Debt (Alternate)

{client_first_name} {client_last_name}

{client_address}

{creditor_name}

{creditor_address}

{creditor_city}, {creditor_state} {creditor_zip}

Re: Remove Inaccurate Information from my Credit Reports. Account #{account_number}

{curr_date}

To Whom It May Concern,

This letter is a formal complaint that you are reporting inaccurate and incomplete credit information.

I am distressed that you have included the information below in my credit profile and that you have failed to maintain reasonable procedures in your operations to assure maximum possible accuracy in the credit reports you publish. Credit reporting laws ensure that bureaus report only 100% accurate credit information. Every step must be taken to assure the information reported is completely accurate and correct. The following information therefore needs to be re-investigated.

Account #{account_number}

{dispute_item_and_explanation}

I respectfully request to be provided proof of this alleged item, specifically the contract, note or other instrument bearing my signature.

Failing that, the item must be deleted from the report as soon as possible. The listed item is entirely inaccurate and incomplete, and as such represents a very serious error in your reporting. Please delete this misleading information and supply a corrected credit profile to all creditors who have received a copy within the last six months, or the last two years for employment purposes.

Additionally, please provide the name, address, and telephone number of each credit grantor or other subscriber.

Under federal law, you have thirty (30) days to complete your re-investigation. Be advised that the description of the procedure used to determine the accuracy and completeness of the information is hereby requested as well, to be provided within fifteen (15) days of the completion of your re-investigation.

Sincerely,

{client_signature}

_____

{client_first_name} {client_last_name

Validation of Debt (Alternate 2)

{client_first_name} {client_last_name}

{client_address}

{creditor_name}

{creditor_address}

{creditor_city}, {creditor_state} {creditor_zip}

{curr_date}

Re: Account #{account_number}

To Whom It May Concern,

This letter is a formal complaint that you are reporting inaccurate and incomplete credit information. I am distressed that you have included the information below in my credit profile and that you have failed to maintain reasonable procedures in your operations to assure maximum possible accuracy in the credit reports you publish.

Credit reporting laws ensure that bureaus report only 100% accurate credit information. Every step must be taken to assure the information reported is completely accurate and correct.

The following information therefore needs to be re-investigated:

{dispute_item_and_explanation}

I respectfully request to be provided proof of this alleged item, specifically the contract, note or other instrument bearing my signature. Failing that, the item must be deleted from the report as soon as possibleThe listed item is entirely inaccurate and incomplete, and as such represents a very serious error in your reporting. Please delete this misleading information and supply a corrected credit profile to all creditors who have received a copy within the last six months, or the last two years for employment purposes.

Additionally, please provide the name, address, and telephone number of each credit grantor or other subscriber.

Under federal law, you have thirty (30) days to complete your re-investigation. Be advised that the description of the procedure used to determine the accuracy and completeness of the information is hereby requested as well, to be provided within fifteen (15) days of the completion of your re-investigation.

Sincerely,

{client_signature}

_____

{client_first_name} {client_last_name}

Validation of Debt (Alternate 3)

{client_first_name} {client_last_name}

{client_address}

{creditor_name}

{creditor_address}

{creditor_city}, {creditor_state} {creditor_zip}

{curr_date}

Re: Acct # {account_number}

To Whom It May Concern:

I am sending this letter to you in response to the notice I received from you on (date of letter). Please be advised that this is not a refusal to pay, but a notice sent pursuant to the Fair Debt Collection Practices Act, 15 USC 1692g Sec. 809 (b) that your claim is disputed and validation is requested.

This is NOT a request for 'verification' or proof of my mailing address, but a request for 'VALIDATION' made pursuant to the above named Title and Section. I respectfully request that your office provide me with factual evidence that I have any legal obligation to pay you.

Please provide me with the following:

-What the money you say I owe is for;

-Explain and show me how you calculated what you say I owe;

-Provide me with copies of any papers that show I agreed to pay what you say I owe;

-Provide a verification or copy of any judgment if applicable;

-Identify the original creditor;

-Prove the Statute of Limitations has not expired on this account;

-Show me that you are licensed to collect in my state; and

-Provide me with your license numbers and Registered Agent.

If your offices have reported invalidated information to any of the three major Credit Bureau's (Equifax, Experian or TransUnion), said action might constitute fraud under both Federal and State Laws. Due to this fact, if any negative mark is found on any of my credit reports by your company or the company that you represent I will not hesitate to bring legal action against you for the following:

-Violation of the Fair Credit Reporting Act

-Violation of the Fair Debt Collection Practices Act

-Defamation of Character

If your offices are able to provide the proper documentation as requested, I will require at least 30 days to investigate this information and during such time all collection activity must cease and desist.

Also during this validation period, if any action is taken which could be considered detrimental to any of my credit reports, I will consult with my legal counsel. This includes any information to a credit reporting repository that could be inaccurate or invalidated or verifying an account as accurate when in fact there is no provided proof that it is.

If your offices fail to respond to this validation request within 30 days from the date of your receipt, all references to this account must be deleted and completely removed from my credit file and a copy of such deletion request shall be sent to me immediately.

I would also like to request, in writing, that no telephone contact be made by your offices to my home or to my place of employment. If your offices attempt telephone communication with me, including but not limited to computer generated calls or correspondence sent to any third parties, it will be considered harassment and I will have no choice but to file suit. All future communications with me MUST be done in writing and sent to the address noted in this letter.

This is an attempt to correct your records, any information obtained shall be used for that purpose.

Kind regards,

{client_signature}

_____

{client_first_name} {client_last_name}

Validation of Debt (Alternate 4)

{client_first_name} {client_last_name}

{client_address}

{creditor_name}

{creditor_address}

{creditor_city} {creditor_state} {creditor_zip}

{curr_date}

Re: {account_number}

To Whom It May Concern,

I am in receipt of your letter claiming that I owe your company for a debt. According to the Federal Fair Debt Collection Practices Act, I have a right to have the alleged debt validated by you.

I have to date, received no proof that I owe your company any debt and I am requesting that you forward to me full and proper documentation as evidence of this alleged debt. As per the FDCPA, it is a violation for any debt collector to pursue collection activity on an account without notifying the debtor in writing within 5 days after any communication. Additionally I am allowed 30 days to dispute the validity of the debt. If you are unable to provide me with proper proof then you must stop attempting to collect this alleged debt.

If you continue to claim I owe a debt that you cannot confirm with proof then you will be in direct violation of the FDCPA. Additionally, any attempt on your part to report this alleged debt to my credit reports will be a violation of the Fair Credit Reporting Act.

Please forward your documentation to me upon receipt of this certified letter. Please note that proper documentation is not a print out or bill from you but rather actual proof of the debt's existence.

Sincerely,

{client_signature}

_____

{client_first_name} {client_last_name}

Validation of Debt (After Dispute to Bureau)

{client_first_name} {client_last_name}

{client_address}

{creditor_name}

{creditor_address}

{creditor_city} {creditor_state} {creditor_zip}

{curr_date}

Re: Account #{account_number}

To Whom It May Concern:

Your company is reporting the below referenced account on my credit report as a collection account.

{dispute_item_and_explanation}

I have disputed this item with the credit reporting agency and they reported you confirmed the account as valid.

In a good faith effort to resolve the matter amicably, I must demand proof of this debt, specifically the alleged contract or other instrument bearing my signature, as well as proof of your authority in this matter. Absent such proof, you must correct any erroneous reports of this past debt as mine.

I am writing to request that you please provide the following information:

1. Please evidence your authorization under 15 USC 1692(e) and 15 USC 1692(f) in this alleged matter.

2. What is your authorization of law for your collection of information?

3. What is your authorization of law for your collection of this alleged debt?

4. Please evidence your authorization to do business or operate in this state.

5. Please evidence proof of the alleged debt, including the alleged contract or other instrument bearing my signature.

6. Please provide a complete account history, including any charges added for collection activity.

You have thirty (30) days from receipt of this notice to respond. Failure to respond in writing, hand-signed, and in a timely manner, will be considered a waiver to any and all of your claims in this matter, and will entitle me to presume you placed this on my credit report(s) in error and that this matter is permanently closed. Provide the proof, or correct the record and remove this invalid debt from all sources to which you have reported it.

For the purposes of 15 USC 1692 et seq., this Notice has the same effect as a dispute to the validity of the alleged debt and a dispute to the validity of your claims. This Notice is an attempt to correct your records, and any information received from you will be collected as evidence should further action be necessary. This is a request for information only, and is not a statement, election, or waiver of status.

{client_first_name} {client_last_name} (DO NOT SIGN)

Validation of Debt (Estoppel by Silence)

***************Instructions Delete these before saving and sending***************

Doctrine of Estoppel by Silence can be extremely powerful with collection agencies that have ignored your Validation of Debt requests. According to Black Law, the meaning is: Estoppel: A legally imposing bar resulting from one's own conduct and precluding any denial assertion regarding a fact. A doctrine that prevents a person from adopting an inconsistent position, attitude or action if it will result in injury to another. An affirmative defense alleging good faith. Estoppel by Silence: Estoppel that arises when a party is under a duty to speak but fails to. The Estoppel letter is used when you request Validation of Debt and do not get a response from the Collection Agency. It uses the "Doctrine of Estoppel" which tells the collection agency that their silence must mean they agree with you. This letter can be used after you have already sent two Validation of Debt requests to a collection agency.

***************Instructions Delete these before saving and sending***************

{client_first_name} {client_last_name}

{client_address}

{creditor_name}

{creditor_address}

{creditor_city}, {creditor_state} {creditor_zip}

{curr_date}

Re: Account number: {account_number}

To Whom It May Concern:

This certified letter, receipt number: _____ is to formally advise you that I believe your company has violated several of my consumer rights. Specifically:

You failed to validate a debt at my request, which is a FDCPA violation and you continued to report a disputed debt to the Credit Bureaus: another FCRA violation

Not only have you ignored my prior requests for validation of debt (proof attached: receipt copies or letter copies) but you continue to report this debt to the credit bureaus causing damage to my character. This letter will again request that you follow the FDCPA and please provide the following:

Validation of Debt Request

-Proof of your right to own/collect this alleged debt

-Balance claimed including all fees, interest and penalties

-Contract bearing my personal signature

As you may be aware, "Estoppel by Silence" legally means that you had a duty to speak but failed to do so therefore, that must mean you agree with me that this debt is false. I will use the Estoppel in my defense.

I expect to receive the proof requested above within 15 days of this letter. Should you again ignore my request for validation of debt I reserve the right to sue your company for violations of my consumer rights as specified under both the FDCPA and the FCRA. I may also seek damages from you if warranted.

Kind regards,

{client_signature}

_____

{client_first_name} {client_last_name}

Validation of Debt (Admission by Silence)

***************Instructions Delete these before saving and sending***************

This letter is similar to the Estoppel by Silence letter. This "Admission by Silence" will advise a collection agency of the Black Law Legal Meaning: The failure of a party to speak after an assertion of fact by another party that, if untrue, would naturally compel a person to deny the statement. This is a powerful statement! If you are right, you speak up; if you are wrong you do nothing to stand your ground. Asserting this information can cause a collections agent to think twice about who they are dealing with and to either prove it or lose it. This is a valuable Validation of Debt tool.

***************Instructions Delete these before saving and sending***************

{client_first_name} {client_last_name}

{client_address}

{creditor_name}

{creditor_address}

{creditor_city}, {creditor_state} {creditor_zip}

{curr_date}

Re: Account number: {account_number}

To Whom It May Concern:

This certified letter, receipt number: XXXXXXXXXXXX is to formally advise you that I believe your company has violated my consumer rights in the following ways.

Specifically you: [list all that apply]

- Failed to validate a debt at my request- FDCPA violation

- Continued to report a disputed debt to the CRA- FCRA violation

- Continued to attempt to collect a disputed debt- FDCPA violation

- Ignored my cease and desist- FDCPA violation

Not only have you ignored my prior requests for validation of debt (see enclosed copies of receipts letters) but you also continue to report this debt to the credit bureaus causing damage to my character. This letter will again request that you follow guidelines of The Fair Debt Collection Practices Act (FDCPA), 15 U.S.C. § 1692 and please provide the following:

Validation of Debt Request

- Proof of your right to own/collect this alleged debt -Balance claimed including all fees, interest and penalties

-Contract bearing my personal signature -License proof to collect debts in my state

As you certainly are aware, "Admission by Silence" means that you had a legal duty to defend your position but failed to do so and if my claims were untrue you would have been compelled to deny my charges. I will use the Admission by Silence in my defense should I be summoned to court or take action against you.

I expect to receive proof requested above, within 15 days of this letter. Should you continue to ignore my request for this validation of debt I reserve the right to sue your company for violations of my consumer rights as indicated under both the FDCPA and the FCRA. I may also seek damages from you if warranted.

Kind regards,

{client_signature}

_____

{client_first_name} {client_last_name}

Validation of Debt with Creditor Disclosure Statement

{client_first_name} {client_last_name}

{client_address}

{client_previous_address}

{creditor_name}

{creditor_address}

{creditor_city} {creditor_state} {creditor_zip}

{creditor_phone}

{curr_date}

Certified Mail No.: _____

Re: Inquiry dated ___: account no. {account_number}

To Whom It May Concern,

Thank you for your inquiry. This is not a refusal to pay, but a notice that I am disputing your claim and I am requesting validation made pursuant to the Fair Debt Collection Practices Act.

Please complete and return the attached disclosure request form.

Understand that I am not requesting a "verification" that you have my mailing address, I am requesting a "validation of debt;" i.e.; competent and valid evidence that I have some contractual obligation to pay you.

You may be aware that sending unsubstantiated demands for payment through the United States Mail System might constitute mail fraud under federal and state law. As such, you may wish to consult with a legal adviser before your next communication with me.

Your failure to satisfy this request within the requirements stated in the Fair Debt Collection Practices Act will be construed as your absolute waiver of any and all claims against me, and your tacit agreement to compensate me for costs and attorney fees.

{client_first_name} {client_last_name} (DO NOT SIGN)

CREDITOR DISCLOSURE STATEMENT

Name and Address of Collector (assignee):_____

Name and Address of Debtor:_____

Account Number(s):_____

What are the terms of assignment for this account? You may attach a facsimile of any records relating to such terms.

Have any insurance claims been made by any creditor or assignee regarding this account? Yes / no

Has the purported balanced of this account been used in any tax deduction claim? Yes / no

Please list the exact products or/or services sold by the collector to the debtor and the dollar amount of each:

Upon failure or refusal of collector to validate this collection action, collector agrees to waive all claims against the debtor named herein and pay debtor for all costs and attorney fees involved in defending this collection action.

X_____

Authorized signature for Collector Date

_____

Printed name

Please return this completed form and attach all assignment or other transfer agreements that would establish your right to collect this debt.

Your claim cannot be considered if any portion of this form is not completed and returned with the required documents. This is a request for validation made pursuant to the Fair Debt Collection Practices Act. If you do not respond as required by this law, your claim will not be considered and you may be liable for damages for continued collection efforts.

Validation of Debt with Creditor Disclosure Statement (Alternate)

{client_first_name} {client_last_name}

{client_address}

{client_previous_address}

{creditor_name}

{creditor_address}

{creditor_city} {creditor_state} {creditor_zip}

{creditor_phone}

{curr_date}

To Whom It May Concern:

This letter is sent to you in response to a notice sent to me on (Date) or in response to a listing on my credit report (CHOOSE THE ONE APPROPRIATE FOR YOUR SPECIFIC SITUATION). Be advised that this is not a refusal to pay, but a notice sent pursuant to the Fair Debt Collection Practices Act, 15 USC 1692g Sec. 809 (8), stating your claim is disputed and validation is requested.

This is NOT a request for "verification" or proof of my mailing address, but a request for VALIDATION made pursuant to the above named Title and Section. I respectfully request your offices provide me with competent evidence that I have any legal obligation to pay you.

At this time I will also inform you that if your offices have reported invalidated information to any of the 3 major Credit Bureaus (Equifax, Experian or TransUnion) this action might constitute fraud under both Federal and State Laws. Due to this fact, if any negative mark is found on any of my credit reports by your company or the company that you represent, I will not hesitate in bringing legal action against you and your client for the following:

Violation of the Fair Credit Reporting Act

Violation of the Fair Debt Collection Practices Act

Defamation of Character

If your offices are able to provide the proper documentation as requested in the following Declaration, I will require at least 30 days to investigate this information, during which time all collection activity must cease and desist. Also during this validation period, if any action is taken which could be considered detrimental to any of my credit reports, I will consult with my legal counsel for suit. This includes any listing of any information to a credit reporting repository that could be inaccurate or invalidated. If your office fails to respond to this validation request within 30 days from the date of your receipt, all references to this account must be deleted and completely removed from my credit file and a copy of such deletion request shall be sent to me immediately.

(OPTIONAL CEASE & DESIST) I would also like to request, in writing, that no further telephone contact be made by your offices to my home or to my place of employment. If your offices continue to attempt telephone communication with me it will be considered harassment and I will have no choice but to file suit. All future communications with me MUST be done in writing and sent to the address noted in this letter. It would be advisable that you and your client assure that your records are in order before I am forced to take legal action.

Best Regards,

{client_first_name} {client_last_name} (DO NOT SIGN)

CREDITOR/DEBT COLLECTOR DECLARATION

Please provide all of the following information and submit the appropriate forms and paperwork within 30 days from the date of your receipt of this request for validation.

_____

Name and Address of Alleged Creditor:

_____

Name on File of Alleged Debtor:

_____

Alleged Account #:

_____

Address on File for Alleged Debtor:

_____

Amount of alleged debt:

_____

Date that this alleged debt became payable:

_____

Date of original charge off or delinquency:

_____

Was this debt assigned to debt collector or purchased?

_____

Amount paid if debt was purchased:

_____

Commission for debt collector if collection efforts are successful:

Please attach a copy of the agreement with your client that grants (Collection Agency Name) the authority to collect this alleged debt.

Also, please attach a copy of any signed agreement debtor has made with debt collector, or other verifiable proof debtor has a contractual obligation to pay debt collector.

Please attach a copy of any agreement that bears the signature of debtor, wherein he/she agreed to pay creditor.

Please attach copies of all statements while this account was open.

Have any insurance claims been made by any creditor regarding this account? YES or NO (circle one)

Have any judgments been obtained by any creditor regarding this account? YES or NO (circle one)

Please provide the name and address of the bonding agent for (Name Of Debt Collector), in case legal action becomes necessary:

_____

_____

_____

_____

Authorized Signature For Creditor Date

_____

Print Name

You must return this completed form along with copies of all requested information, assignments or other transfer agreements, which would establish your right to collect this alleged debt within 30 days from the date of your receipt of this letter. Your claim cannot and WILL NOT be considered if any portion of this form is not completed and returned with copies of all requested documents. This is a request for validation made pursuant to the Fair Debt Collection Practices Act. Please allow 30 days for processing after I receive this information back.

Validation of Debt with Creditor Disclosure Statement) (Alternate 2)

{client_first_name} {client_last_name}   .

{client_address}

{client_previous_address}

{creditor_name}

{creditor_address}

{creditor_city} {creditor_state} {creditor_zip}

{creditor_phone}

{curr_date}

To Whom It May Concern:

Re: Acct # XXXX-XXXX-XXXX-XXXX

To Whom It May Concern:

This letter is sent to you in response to a notice sent to me on (Date) or in response to a listing on my credit report (CHOOSE THE ONE APPROPRIATE FOR YOUR SPECIFIC SITUATION). This is not a refusal to pay, but a notice that your claim is disputed.

Pursuant to the Fair Debt Collection Practices Act, 15 USC 1692g Sec. 809 (8) (FDCPA), I have the right to request validation of the debt you say I owe you. I am requesting proof that I am indeed the party you are asking to pay this debt, and there is some contractual obligation which is binding on me to pay this debt.

Your attorney or legal staff will agree that compliance with this request is required under State and Federal Statutes.

In addition to the questionnaire below, please attach copies of:

Agreement with your client that grants you the authority to collect on this alleged debt, or proof of acquisition by purchase or assignment.

Agreement that bears the signature of the alleged debtor wherein he or she agreed to pay the creditor.

Also, please be advised this letter is not only a formal dispute, but a request for you to cease and desist any and all collection activities.

I require compliance with the terms and conditions of this letter within 30 days. or a complete withdrawal, in writing, of any claim.

In the event of noncompliance, I reserve the right to file charges and/or complaints with appropriate County, State & Federal authorities ,the BBB and State Bar associations for violations of the FDCPA, FCRA, and Federal and State statutes on fraudulent extortion .

I also hereby reserve my right to take private civil action against you to recover damages.

Sincerely,

{client_first_name} {client_last_name} (DO NOT SIGN)

DEBT VALIDATION FORM

Please provide all of the following information and submit the appropriate forms and paperwork within 30 days from the date of your receipt of this request for validation.

Account #: _____

Original Creditor's Name:

_____

Name of Debtor:

_____

Address of Debtor:

_____

Balance of Account:

_____

Date you acquired this debt:

_____

This Debt was: assigned ___ purchased ___

Please indicate the credit bureaus which you have reported this account to:

Experian: _____

Equifax: _____

TransUnion: _____

Other: _____

Validation of Medical Debt (HIPAA Request)

***************Instructions delete these before saving and sending***************

Since A large percentage of collection debts are medical related, this letter will assist you to validate a medical debt from a collection agency by referencing the HIPAA law. HIPAA stands for HEALTH INSURANCE PORTABILITY AND ACCOUNTABILITY ACT and it protects your privacy by preventing your medical records from being given to third parties without your written consent. The HIPAA law allows you to question your privacy while validating a medical debt and may also suspend reporting the collection item to your credit reports until it is resolved. Make sure that you understand the HIPAA requirements before using this letter. If they have violated HIPAA, this letter may assist you in deleting a medical collections account along with any mention of it on your credit reports!

***************Instructions delete these before saving and sending***************

{client_first_name} {client_last_name}

{client_address}

{creditor_name}

{creditor_address}

{creditor_city}, {creditor_state} {creditor_zip}

{curr_date}

Amount of debt: Date of Service: Provider of Service:

To Whom It May Concern,

I received a bill from you on [insert date] and as allowable under the Fair Debt Collections Practices Act, I am requesting validation of the alleged debt. I am aware that there is a debt from [name of doctor, hospital, clinic, etc.] but I am unaware of the amount due and your bill does not include a detailed breakdown of any fees.

Furthermore, I am allowed under the HIPAA law (Health Insurance Portability and Accountability Act of 1996) to protect my privacy and medical records from third parties. I do not recall giving permission to [name of provider] for them to release my medical information to a third party. I understand that the HIPAA does allow for limited information about me but any details may only be revealed with the patients authorization, therefore my request is twofold and as follows:

Validation of Debt and HIPAA authorization

- Please provide a breakdown of fees including any and all collection costs and medical charges

- Please provide a copy of my signature with the provider of service to release my medical information to you

- Immediately cease any credit bureau reporting until debt has been validated by me

Please send this information to my address listed above and accept this letter, sent certified mail, as my formal debt validation request, of which I am allowed under the FDCPA.

Please note that withholding the information you received from any medical provider in an attempt to be HIPAA compliant will be a violation of the FDCPA because you will be deceiving me after my written request. I am requesting full documentation of what you received from the provider of service in connection with this alleged debt.

Furthermore, any reporting of this debt to the credit bureaus prior to allowing me to validate it may be a violation of the Fair Credit Reporting Act, which can allow me to seek damages from a collection agent.

I await your reply with the above requested proof. Upon receiving it, I will correspond back with you by certified mail.

Kind regards,

{client_signature}

_____

{client_first_name} {client_last_name}

Goodwill Letter sent to Original Creditor

***************Instructions delete these before saving and sending***************

This This letter can be used with a creditor as an attempt to have them remove negative information from your reports, especially if you have been a good customer for many years and only have minor negative marks on your record with them.

***************Instructions delete these before saving and sending***************

{client_first_name} {client_last_name}

{client_address}

{creditor_name}

{creditor_address}

{creditor_city}, {creditor_state} {creditor_zip}

{curr_date}

Re: Account number: (Account number)

To Whom It May Concern,

I was advised to write to you by your customer service department concerning my credit rating with your company. I have enjoyed a credit account with (company name) for many years. During the course of our business association, I have honored and respected my account agreement to the fullest. I appreciate how wonderful your service has always been.

Unfortunately, 2 years ago, I was in a financial dilemma due to (job loss, health issues, new baby, etc.). As a result 3 of my payments to you were delayed. Because your account with me is extremely important I managed to borrow the money to cover the late payments. I paid those payments 30 days late on three occasions over a nine-month period but I made sure to fulfill my obligation to ensure that your company suffered no loss.

I am thankful and appreciative for the years of positive credit history that I have obtained through your company but now those 3 late marks on my credit reports are causing me tremendous stress. I am trying to move up to a better paid position at my work, but the negative remarks are hurting my efforts.

This is where my "Goodwill Request" comes in. I desperately need this promotion and I would be extremely appreciative if you would please complete a UDF - Universal Data Form and fax it to the credit bureaus to remove those entries.

The credit bureaus have advised me that they will report anything as instructed to by you, but they need to have that instruction in writing. I beg that you may help me and take into consideration how good of a customer I have been and how long I have had an account with you.

Kind regards,

{client_signature}

_____

{client_first_name} {client_last_name}

Goodwill Adjustment Letter

{client_first_name} {client_last_name}

{client_address}

{creditor_name}

{creditor_address}

{creditor_city}, {creditor_state} {creditor_zip}

{curr_date}

Re: Account number: (Account number)

To Whom It May Concern,

I have received my credit report, from (Credit Bureau Name). I have contacted (Creditor's name) numerous times and even disputed it with the Credit Bureau. I am requesting a goodwill adjustment to remove the late payment(s) in order to refinance my home. I know this request is unusual, but it is ruining my good credit standing. I have had a mishap, and realize things happen. If you look at my records, I was always on time. The late payment(s) is reported to Equifax bureau and I am requesting removal of these two late payments, as it has been reported to the bureau's.

Also, the account has been paid and closed for (insert number of years closed), why is this reflecting, on my credit report? Is there interest that I am unaware of?

Sincerely,

{client_signature}

_____

{client_first_name} {client_last_name}

Inform a Creditor that you have filed for Bankruptcy

{client_first_name} {client_last_name}

{client_address}

{curr_date}

Re: [Company] v. [Client's first and last name] [Account Number] Balance: $XXX

To Whom It May Concern,

Please be advised that I filed a voluntary petition pursuant to Chapter 7 of the Bankruptcy Code. The bankruptcy case number is _____ and it was filed on _____ with you listed as one of my creditors.

To my knowledge, have never had non-sufficient funds and I am not aware of any negative entries. Kindly forward me a copy of my InformCreditorforBankruptcy record so that I may verify its accuracy.

Pursuant to 11 U.S.C. Section 362(a), you are automatically stayed by the filing of this petition from taking any action to collect any debt from me or from enforcing any lien against me. A violation of the stay may be actionable pursuant to 362(h) or as contempt of court and punishable accordingly.

Attorney name: _____

Attorney address: _____

Attorney phone number: _____

Kind regards,

{client_signature}

_____

{client_first_name} {client_last_name}

Inform Creditor of Bankruptcy

{client_first_name} {client_last_name}

{client_address}

{creditor_name}

{creditor_address}

{creditor_city}, {creditor_state} {creditor_zip}

{curr_date}

Re: Account number: (ENTER ACCOUNT NUMBER)

To Whom It May Concern:

Please cease and desist all collection activities you have begun or are considering to take against me. I plan on filing a petition in bankruptcy court in the coming months.

Sincerely yours,

{client_signature}

_____

{client_first_name} {client_last_name}

{Reaffirming Debt After Bankruptcyclient_first_name} {client_last_name}

{client_address}

{creditor_name}

{creditor_address}

{creditor_city} {creditor_state} {creditor_zip}

Attn: (name of person you are speaking with)

{curr_date}

Re: Reaffirmation of Debt

Dear (name of person you are speaking with)

This letter acknowledges and reaffirms to (CREDITOR/FURNISHER), its successors and assignees, that in regards to a certain prior discharged debt, the undersigned agrees to remain bound on this debt in the amount of $(AMOUNT OWED; to the same extent as if the debt was not discharged in the first place.

I agree to pay this debt in the following manner:

[PROVIDE DETAILS OF THE MANNER THIS WILL BE PAID, TERMS, DOLLAR AMOUNT, ETC.]

This agreement is binding and I understand what a debt reaffirmation is.

{client_signature}

_____

{client_first_name} {client_last_name}   Date

(Debtor)

In the presence of:

_____

(Witness)

Notary Seal (optional)

Agreement Offer Settlement to Dismiss Judgment

***************Instructions delete these before saving and sending***************

Here is an effective settlement offer to a creditor to settle and dismiss a judgment

***************Instructions delete these before saving and sending***************

{client_first_name} {client_last_name}

{client_address}

{creditor_name}

{creditor_address}

{creditor_city}, {creditor_state} {creditor_zip}

Re: Judgment - Case number: XXXXXXXXXXXX Judgment amount: $XXXXX

{curr_date}

To Whom It May Concern,

Dear Sir,

I am aware of the funds due to you and of the judgment placed against me for those funds. I had every intention of taking care of this prior to the entry of the judgment, but unfortunately time constraints made that impossible for me.

Today, I am writing to you in the hope that we may put this matter behind us and settle out the judgment for good, under a few conditions. This will save you both time and money trying to collect the judgment and will help me to recover from your negative entry in my credit history reports.

I have been offered a loan from a close family member to pay you (amount you are offering) to settle the debt in-full and have the judgment dismissed.

As the judgment creditor, you reserve the right to dismiss or vacate the judgment as well as entering it. If I pay you from this offer letter saving you immense time, paperwork and fees, you can then file a simple paper with the courts dismissing the judgment.

My offer is to pay you (amount you are offering) in exchange for the dismissal so that we have both gained something from this unfortunate situation. It is extremely important that you dismiss the judgment rather than satisfying it. The reason behind my request is because a satisfied judgment looks no better on my credit report than a filed judgment. If you agree to dismiss this judgment I can justify payment.

Upon your signed approval of this offer, I will forward the full settlement funds to you immediately. I understand this offer is void if I do not send you $_____ within 5-10 days of your signed confirmation.

If you agree to "dismiss" the judgment upon receiving my full and final payment of $_____, then please sign this offer and acceptance.

Sincerely,

{client_signature}

_____

{client_first_name} {client_last_name}

Date signed _____

I agree and accept this offer,

_____

Judgment creditor signature

_____

Judgment creditor name

Date signed _____

Agreement to Dismiss Court Judgment

***************Instructions delete these before saving and sending***************

If you have been successful in getting a creditor to agree to dismissing a judgment, congratulations on a huge accomplishment! - Here is the letter you need to complete and finalize the deal.

***************Instructions delete these before saving and sending***************

{client_first_name} {client_last_name}

{client_address}

{creditor_name}

{creditor_address}

{creditor_city}, {creditor_state} {creditor_zip}

Re: Account number

{curr_date}

To Whom It May Concern,

Court Name and Location:

Judgment Creditor:

Judgment Debtor:

Case Number: Amount of Judgment: Date of Entry:

We the undersigned Judgment Creditor and Judgment Debtor have both agreed to settle this matter and hereby jointly apply to the court for an order that this judgment involved (court case number and date entered) shall be set aside and dismissed.

Signed:

Judgment Credit: _____ Judgment Debtor: _____

Name (printed): _____ Name (printed): _____

Date signed: _____ Date signed: _____

Judgment Proof letter

***************Instructions delete these before saving and sending***************

You may be judgment proof if you are retired, disabled, unemployed or on welfare. - A creditor will often consider these facts before wasting time and money in coming after you. If you have the ability to offer any proof to show that you are "judgment proof," enclose it with your letter. If you are unsure and think you may be sued, we suggest contacting a qualified attorney in your state to see your options. If you honestly are judgment proof, most creditors will not waste the expense of taking you to court.

***************Instructions delete these before saving and sending***************

{client_first_name} {client_last_name}

{client_address}

{creditor_name}

{creditor_address}

{creditor_city}, {creditor_state} {creditor_zip}

{curr_date}

Re: Account number / Debtor's name

To Whom It May Concern,

Please be advised that I have received your letter requesting money for the above debt. This letter, sent certified mail, receipt number_____ is to formally advise you that I cannot pay this debt and have no attachable income or assets to levy.

I believe that I am judgment proof and I can prove it if necessary in a court of law. Should you attempt to file suit against me I will provide the court with valid proof of my situation.

My circumstances are that I am judgment proof because :

(list reasons:) I have no assets, no home or car (to attach), no income and no prospects and; I am disabled, unemployed, on social security or welfare.

I understand the debt is due, however your repeated attempts to collect are causing me much stress and therefore I must also ask you to cease and desist you (if the account is being pursued by a third party debt collector). If my situation changes, I will contact you immediately.

Kind regards,

{client_signature}

_____

{client_first_name} {client_last_name}

Judgment Proof Letter (Alternate)

{client_first_name} {client_last_name}

{client_address}

{creditor_name}

{creditor_address}

{creditor_city}, {creditor_state} {creditor_zip}

{curr_date}

Re: Account number: {account_number} - Request for Reduced Payments

To Whom It May Concern:

Due to my desperate financial situation, I am unable to make payments on my account as originally agreed. My financial position is as follows:

(STATE REASON; FINANCIAL, MEDICAL, DISABILITY, UNEMPLOYED, ETC.)

I cannot work sufficient hours to meet my current expenses. My only sources of income are the following:

(LIST SOURCES OF INCOME)

I am familiar with the law and have been advised that I am "judgment proof." If I should file for bankruptcy, I will claim all of my property as exempt. If you sue me and obtain judgment, you will not be able to collect any of my property to satisfy the judgment.

Please cease all collection activities you have taken or are considering. While I will absolutely present you with reasonable financial or medical information, I must avoid stress (including high-pressure collections activity and lawsuits).

I promise to inform you immediately should my financial condition improve and I am able to resume sending you normal payments.

Thank you for your consideration and understanding.

Sincerely yours,

{client_signature}

_____

{client_first_name} {client_last_name}

Request Original Creditor to Take Back Debt from Collection Agency

***************Instructions delete these before saving and sending***************

This can be a very useful letter if you have a collection agency that has been abusive to you for a valid debt. Even if you owe the balance and do not contest the debt, it's often a good idea to inform the Original Creditor that the Collection Agency was abusive, misleading or simply too aggressive and that you refuse to communicate with them any longer. If the Collections Agent did violate the law, the Original Creditor will be very motivated to take pull back your account to avoid trouble. Once the Original Creditor takes back the account, the Collections listing will be deleted from your credit history reports

***************Instructions delete these before saving and sending***************

{client_first_name} {client_last_name}

{client_address}

{creditor_name}

{creditor_address}

{creditor_city}, {creditor_state} {creditor_zip}

{curr_date}

Re: Amount of debt: XXXXX Original creditor: XXXXXXXXXXXXXX Collection agency: XXXXXXXXXXXXXX Account ID: XXXXXXXXXXXXXX

To Whom It May Concern,

On (insert date) you assigned my debt to (collection agency name). Since that time I believe they have violated the Fair Debt Collection Practices Act.

Specifically, violations are: (List all violations: called late at night, refused to allow you to validate it, told other third parties about your debt, left harassing telephone messages, refused to provide proof, harassed or intimidated you, etc. Be sure to include any proof you have).

I am aware that I had an outstanding debt with your company but I refuse to make any arrangements with a collection agency, particularly one that does not respect my rights. Now that they have violated the FDCPA, I am requesting to communicate directly with you, otherwise I may be forced to take legal action against this collection agency that represents you.

Please reply by mail to advise me if you will take the account back so that I may make arrangements with you. Upon receiving your reply I will immediately contact you.

I have forwarded a copy of this letter to the collection agency and I am including a cease and desist clause directed towards that agency. From this moment forward I will only correspond with you.

I await your reply. Upon receiving it, I will write back to you via certified mail.

Kind regards,

{client_signature}_____

{client_first_name} {client_last_name}

Certified mail receipt number:

Warning of VOD refusal and FDCPA violations

{client_first_name} {client_last_name}

{client_address}

{creditor_name}

{creditor_address}

{creditor_city} {creditor_state} {creditor_zip}

{curr_date}

Re: {account_number}

To Whom It May Concern,

Please be apprised that you are in direct violation of the Fair Debt Collections Practices Act. In my opinion you have violated at least three sections of this act by:

Failing to validate a debt as allowed to the debtor under 15 USC 1692 (g) Section 809 (b)

Communicating with a debtor after receiving a cease and desist certified mail under 15 USC 1692 (g) Section 805 (c)

Harassment of alleged debtor under the "abuse & harassment" subsection of the statute, USC 1692 (g) Section 806 (5)

I have complete and thorough records of your violations and I am prepared to protect myself and my rights from unscrupulous collection agencies.

In (EXACT DATE), I sent by certified mail (receipt number: (CERTIFIED MAIL RECEIPT NUMBER), a request for your office to provide me with proof and evidence of the debt you alleged I owed, and I did so within 30 days of receiving your first notice. In that same letter I also included my cease and desist instructions.

After verified delivery of my letter (via your office's signature), you proceeded to mail a simple bill which is NOT considered a "validation of debt" by any means. You may wish to familiarize yourself with what is required when validating a debt.

Your office also proceeded to contact me by phone after the delivery and acceptance of my certified letter. Contacting a person after a cease and desist can lead to serious trouble for your agency including damages of up to $1000.00 per incident.

I highly doubt that this $(ENTER AMOUNT OF DEBT) debt is worth your agency's license and the fees and penalties for violations of the FDCPA.

There is no question that you willfully violated my rights and that I could bring charges against you immediately. However, I am assuming this has been a terrible mistake on your part and that you will take appropriate steps to enlighten yourself and your staff of such dangerous actions.

I will also be checking my credit report to see if you have willfully reported an unverified and disputable debt to the credit bureaus. If so, that will be a violation of the Fair Credit Reporting Act. I will state again in this certified mailing that you have failed to verify the debt as accurate, you have provided no proof of this alleged debt, and I must remind you again to not contact me in any way via phone or mail in reference to collecting this debt.

If I receive anything other than absolute proof from you, provided by the original creditor, I will assume you are harassing me and ignoring my cease and desist, and I will take action against you for these continued violations and abuse.

Sincerely,

{client_signature}

_____

{client_first_name} {client_last_name}

Warning Violation for Expired Debt Collection {client_first_name} {client_last_name}

{client_address}

{creditor_name}

{creditor_address}

{creditor_city} {creditor_state} {creditor_zip}

{curr_date}

Re: {account_number}

To Whom It May Concern,

In reviewing my credit reports, I came across a debt item that was listed incorrectly. I disputed this account to the credit bureaus and they confirmed it was verified as accurate by you.

I am aware of the rights I have and am requesting that you immediately remove the debt from my credit reports or you may face damages by reporting inaccurate data to a credit reporting agency. (See the FCRA) This debt is listed as a charge off, with a last date of activity of _____. You are reporting the charge off date as the date you purchased the debt instead of the actual charge off date. This is a clear violation of the Fair Credit Reporting Act, as it is clearly stated that "no debt may be reported to a consumers' credit file for any longer than 7 years from the date of first serious delinquency or charge off."

Because you have altered the charge off date as the date you purchased it, you are committing fraud. I have informed the credit bureaus of this, and have asked for a second verification. When that verification comes to you, I suggest you follow the law and report the true facts. In addition to this debt being over the allowed time to report (7 years) it has also passed the statute of limitations to collect. I have no intention of paying this old expired debt and I am informing you of this now.

Should you attempt to report or collect this expired debt, I will contact my Attorney General and fill out a complaint to the Federal Trade Commission, and I will take steps to collect damages from you of up to $1,000.00. I believe I have a case against you for violating sections of the FDCPA and FCRA should you continue.

Sincerely,

{client_signature}

_____

{client_first_name} {client_last_name}

Warning Violation for Expired Debt Collection (Alternate)

{client_first_name} {client_last_name}

{client_address}

{creditor_name}

{creditor_address}

{creditor_city} {creditor_state} {creditor_zip}

{curr_date}

Re: {account_number}

To Whom It May Concern,

Please be advised that you are attempting to collect on an expired debt. I am invoking my right to cease you, based on factual law that this debt in question is legally expired under the Statute of Limitations. Accordingly, I am requesting that you do not attempt to collect this expired debt, and should you seek legal recourse I will invoke my right of the expired statute as a valid defense.

Additionally any attempts to harm my credit history and rating by updating or changing dates after you have been informed that the debt is expired, is a direct violation of the FDCPA. Any abuse to my credit rating on your part will be met with all recourse available to me by the law.

I am aware of how long items may remain on my credit reports and any attempt to extend the reporting time will be investigated by me, and reported to my State Attorney General and the American Collectors Association.

I am completely aware of how long the debt may be legally collectable and how long it may be legally reportable. I realize a debt is allowed to be reported on my credit history for no longer than 7 years, and my research has shown me that often a collection agency will reset the date of original charge off to the date they purchased it, thus trying to extend the reporting time in an attempt to force a consumer into paying it. I am informing you of this knowledge so that you may do the right thing.

I have no intentions of renewing the expired statute of limitations, so please stop wasting your time contacting me. I expect this will be the last time I hear from you.

Sincerely,

{client_signature}

_____

{client_first_name} {client_last_name}

Warning of Expired Statute of Limitations

{client_first_name} {client_last_name}

{client_address}

{creditor_name}

{creditor_address}

{creditor_city} {creditor_state} {creditor_zip}

{curr_date}

RE: Account number {account_number}

To Whom It May Concern,

Please be advised that you are attempting to collect on an expired debt. I am invoking my right to cease you, based on factual law that this debt in question is legally expired under the Statute of Limitations.

Accordingly, I am requesting that you do not attempt to collect this expired debt, and should you seek legal recourse I will invoke my right of the expired statute as a valid defense.

Additionally any attempts to harm my credit rating by updating or changing dates after you have been informed that the debt is expired, are a direct violation of the FDCPA.

Any abuse to my credit rating on your part will be met with all recourse available to me.

I am aware of how long items may remain on my credit reports and any attempt to extend the reporting time will be investigated by me, and reported to the American Collectors Association and my State Attorney General.

I am completely aware of how long the debt is legally collectable and how long it is legally reportable. I realize a debt is allowed to be reported to my credit for 7 years, and my research has shown me that often a collection agency will reset the date of original charge off to the date they purchased it, thus trying to extend the reporting time in an attempt to force a consumer into paying it. I am informing you of this knowledge so that you may do the right thing.

I have no intention of renewing the expired statute of limitations, so please stop wasting your time contacting me.

I expect this will be the last time I hear from you.

Sincerely,

{client_signature}

_____

{client_first_name} {client_last_name}

Pay For Delete (Alternate 3)

{client_first_name} {client_last_name}

{client_address}

{creditor_name}

<CREDITOR/FURNISHER ADDRESS>

Dear Collection Manager:

It has come to my attention through the credit bureaus that you claim I owe a debt to your agency. While I have never had the debt verified to me as legitimate by your agency, I may be willing to save us both some time and effort by "settling the debt out" with restrictions.

I understand that you hold all the rights to report the debt to the credit bureaus as you see fit and you can change that listing at any time, as the source owning the debt. I am sure you are aware of my right to dispute this debt and to request full proof of the obligation as per the FDCPA. Paying this unverified debt means little to me if we cannot mutually agree that you will report the debt as mentioned below.

While I realize that your purpose is to collect debts as a collection agent, I am also aware of what a paid collection on my report would represent for me, which is not favorable. That being said, I know that you have the absolute right to report this debt as you see fit or not report it at all. It is only unlawful to report false information but you may remove a listing any time at your discretion.

Please do not attempt to continue contacting me outside of this offer or I will be forced to cease and desist our communication and request full lengthy verification of the debt. My goal is to arrange a term acceptable to both.

My financial resources are limited and I am trying to do what's right but I am realistic about my financial ability. I will pay your company the amount of $(AMOUNT) as "payment in full" for this account. Upon receipt of the above payment, your company has agreed to delete the item on my credit reports.

If you agree with these terms please acknowledge this letter with your signature and return it to me. You agree that the terms herein are confidential and that you have the authority to make such decisions. No payment will be made without written confirmation from you.

Upon receipt of this signed acknowledgment, I will immediately mail you a cashier's check by priority mail. This is not a renewed promise to pay but rather a restricted offer only. If no terms can be met, no new arrangements will be made and the offer will be void.

_____

Name of collection agency

_____

Signature of company officer:

_____

Name   Title   Date:

Dispute Credit Report Items (Round 1 Alternate)

{client_first_name} {client_last_name}

{client_address}

{client_previous_address}

{t_no}

{bdate}

{ss_number}

{bureau_address}

{curr_date}

Re: Letter to Remove Inaccurate Credit Information: Report #:

To Whom It May Concern:

I received a copy of my credit report and found the following item(s) to be errors. See the attached copy of my credit report; the errors have been highlighted. Here as follows are items in error:

{dispute_item_and_explanation}

By the provisions of the Fair Credit Reporting Act, I demand that these items be investigated and removed from my report. It is my understanding that you will recheck these items with the creditor who has posted them. Please remove any information that the creditor cannot verify. I understand that under 15 U.S.C. Sec. 1681i(a), you must complete this reinvestigation within 30 days of receipt of this letter.

Sincerely yours,

{client_signature}

_____

{client_first_name} {client_last_name}

Dispute Credit Report Items (Round 1 Alternate 2)

{client_first_name} {client_last_name}

{client_address}

{t_no}

{bdate}

{ss_number}

{bureau_address}

{curr_date}

To Whom It May Concern,

This letter is a formal complaint that you are reporting inaccurate and incomplete credit information on my Credit Report.

I understand that mistakes happen but your inaccurate information could cost me in higher interest rates and I have enough expenses as it is. Please investigate the following information and either remove it or at least send me the information that you used to add it to my report.

{dispute_item_and_explanation}

Thank You

Sincerely yours,

{client_signature}

_____

{client_first_name} {client_last_name}

Dispute Credit Report Items (Round 1 Alternate 3)

{client_first_name} {client_last_name}

{client_address}

{t_no}

{bdate}

{ss_number}

{bureau_address}

{curr_date}

To Whom It May Concern,

This letter is a formal complaint that you are reporting inaccurate and incomplete credit information. I am distressed that you have included the information below in my credit profile and that you have failed to maintain reasonable procedures in your operations to assure maximum possible accuracy in the credit reports you publish. Credit reporting laws ensure that bureaus report only 100% accurate credit information. Every step must be taken to assure the information reported is completely accurate and correct. The following information therefore needs to be re-investigated.

{dispute_item_and_explanation}

I respectfully request to be provided proof of this alleged item, specifically the contract, note or other instrument bearing my signature

Failing that, the item must be deleted from the report as soon as possible. This information is entirely inaccurate and incomplete, and as such represents a very serious error in your reporting. Please delete this misleading information and supply a corrected credit profile to all creditors who have received a copy within the last six months, or the last two years for employment purposes.

Additionally, please provide the name, address, and telephone number of each credit grantor or other subscriber.

Under federal law, you have thirty (30) days to complete your re-investigation. Be advised that the description of the procedure used to determine the accuracy and completeness of the information is hereby requested as well, to be provided within fifteen (15) days of the completion of your re-investigation.

Sincerely yours,

{client_signature}

_____

{client_first_name} {client_last_name}

Request Removal after Bureau Investigation

{client_first_name} {client_last_name}

{client_address}

{bdate}

{ss_number}

Credit Report Number:

{bureau_address}

{curr_date}

Re: Removal of Incorrect Items from Credit Report (More than 30 days have passed)

To Whom It May Concern:

On (DATE), I sent you a request to reinvestigate incorrect items which were listed in my credit history report.

{dispute_item_and_explanation}

I am enclosing a photocopy of that original request. The Fair Credit Reporting Act requires that you complete your reinvestigation of my request within 30 days. It has now been more than 30 days.

I will assume that I have not received your reply because you have been unable to verify this information. Please remove this incorrect information at once and send me an updated copy of my credit history report. I also request that you please send notices of corrections to anyone who received my credit report in the past six months.

Thank you time and help in this matter. I have also sent a copy of this letter to the Federal Trade Commission.

Sincerely yours,

{client_signature}

_____

{client_first_name} {client_last_name}

Request Removal after Creditor Verification

{client_first_name} {client_last_name}

{client_address}

{client_previous_address}

{t_no}

{bdate}

{ss_number}

{bureau_address}

{curr_date}

Re: Creditor Verification of incorrect items on my credit history report.

Credit Report Number:

To Whom It May Concern,

On (DATE), I received my credit report from you. It included the following incorrect information:

{dispute_item_and_explanation}

I am enclosing a copy of my credit report with the incorrect data highlighted. I just received a letter from that creditor verifying that this information on my credit report is inaccurate and should be removed from my credit file. I have enclosed a copy of the letter.

OR

On (DATE) I spoke with (CONTACT PERSON) from . This person verified that this information on my credit report is indeed inaccurate and should be removed from my credit file.

{dispute_item_and_explanation}

You can reach this person at (CONTACT NUMBER)

I am enclosing a copy of my credit report with the incorrect data highlighted. This incorrect and negative information is damaging my credit. Please remove this incorrect information at once and send me an updated copy of my credit history report. I also request that you please send notices of corrections to anyone who received my credit report in the past six months.

Thank you for your time and help in this matter.

Sincerely yours,

{client_signature}

_____

{client_first_name} {client_last_name}

cc: Federal Trade Commission

(ENCLOSE A COPY OF CREDIT REPORT WITH THE INCORRECT ITEMS IN QUESTION HIGHLITED. ALSO INCLUDE ALL OTHER DOCUMENTATION VERIFYING THE ABOVE FACTS)

Dispute Follow-up after no response for 30 days

{client_first_name} {client_last_name}

{client_address}

{t_no}

{bdate}

{ss_number}

{bureau_address}

{curr_date}

To Whom It May Concern,

This letter is a formal complaint that you are reporting inaccurate and incomplete credit information.

I am distressed that you have included the information below in my credit profile and that you have failed to maintain reasonable procedures in your operations to assure maximum possible accuracy in the credit reports you publish. Credit reporting laws ensure that bureaus report only 100% accurate credit information. Every step must be taken to assure the information reported is completely accurate and correct. The following information therefore needs to be re-investigated. I respectfully request to be provided proof of this alleged item, specifically the contract, note or other instrument bearing my signature.

{dispute_item_and_explanation}

Failing that, the item must be deleted from the report as soon as possible. The listed item is entirely inaccurate and incomplete, and as such represents a very serious error in your reporting. Please delete this misleading information and supply a corrected credit profile to all creditors who have received a copy within the last six months, or the last two years for employment purposes.

Additionally, please provide the name, address, and telephone number of each credit grantor or other subscriber.

Under federal law, you have thirty (30) days to complete your re-investigation. Be advised that the description of the procedure used to determine the accuracy and completeness of the information is hereby requested as well, to be provided within fifteen (15) days of the completion of your re-investigation.

Sincerely yours,

{client_signature}

_____

{client_first_name} {client_last_name}

Dispute Follow-up after no response for 60 days

{client_first_name} {client_last_name}

{client_address}

{t_no}

{bdate}

{ss_number}

{bureau_address}

{curr_date}

To Whom It May Concern,

This letter is formal notice that you have failed to respond in a timely manner to my dispute letter of insert date, deposited by registered mail with the U.S. Postal Service on that date. Federal law requires you to respond within thirty (30) days, yet you have failed to respond. Failure to comply with these federal regulations by credit reporting agencies are investigated by the Federal Trade Commission (FTC) (see 15 USC 41, et seq.).

I am maintaining a careful record of my communications with you for the purpose of filing a complaint with the FTC should you continue in your non-compliance. I further remind you that, as in Wenger v. Trans Union Corp., No. 95-6445 (C.D.Cal. Nov. 14, 1995), you may be liable for your willful non-compliance.

Be aware that I am making a final goodwill attempt to have you clear up this matter. You have 15 days to cure.

For your benefit, and as a gesture of my goodwill, I will restate my dispute. The following information needs to be verified and, following failure to verify, deleted from the report as soon as possible:

{dispute_item_and_explanation}

The listed item is entirely inaccurate and incomplete, and represents a very serious error in your reporting. Please delete this misleading information and supply a corrected credit profile to all creditors who have received a copy within the last six months, or the last two years for employment purposes.

Additionally, please provide the name, address, and telephone number of each credit grantor or other subscriber.

Under federal law you had thirty (30) days to complete your re-investigation, yet you have failed to respond. Do not delay any further.

Be advised that the description of the procedure used to determine the accuracy and completeness of the information is hereby requested as well, to be provided within fifteen (15) days of the completion of your re-investigation.

Sincerely yours,

{client_signature}

_____

{client_first_name} {client_last_name}

Dispute After Investigation: "The Prove it" Letter

{client_first_name} {client_last_name}

{client_address}

{t_no}

{bdate}

{ss_number}

{bureau_address}

Attn: Customer Relations Department

{curr_date}

To Whom It May Concern,

I am in disagreement with the items listed below which still appear on my credit report, even after your Investigation. I would like these items immediately re-investigated. These inaccuracies are highly injurious to my credit rating.

{dispute_item_and_explanation}

Furthermore, In accordance with The Fair Credit Reporting Act, Public law 91-506, Title VI, Section 611, Subsection A-D, please provide the names and business addresses of each individual with whom you verified the above, so that I may follow up.

Please forward me an updated credit report after you have completed your Investigation and corrections.

Your cooperation and prompt attention are greatly appreciated.

Sincerely yours,

{client_signature}

_____

{client_first_name} {client_last_name}

Request to Describe Investigation Procedures

{client_first_name} {client_last_name}

{client_address}

{t_no}

{bdate}

{ss_number}

{bureau_address}

{curr_date}

To Whom It May Concern,

This letter is a formal request for the description of the procedures used to determine the accuracy and completeness of the disputed information, including the business name, address, and telephone number of any furnisher of information contacted in connection with this reinvestigation.

{dispute_item_and_explanation}

I am disappointed that you have failed to maintain reasonable procedures to assure complete accuracy in the information you publish, and insist you comply with the law by providing the requested information within the 15 days allowed.

As already stated, the listed item is inaccurate and incomplete, and is a very serious error in reporting. Please supply a corrected credit profile to all creditors who have received a copy within the last 6 months, or the last 2 years for employment purposes.

Additionally, please provide the name, address, and telephone number of each credit grantor or other subscriber.

Sincerely,

{client_signature}

{client_first_name} {client_last_name}

Demand to Comply with Investigation Request

{client_first_name} {client_last_name}

{client_address}

{client_previous_address}

{bdate}

{ss_number}

{bureau_address}

Attn.: Consumer Relations

{curr_date}

To Whom It May Concern,

On (DATE), I wrote to you requesting an investigation into items that I believed were (CHOOSE: INNACCURATE, OUTDATED OR OBSOLETE). To date, I have not received a reply from you or any acknowledgment that an investigation has begun. In my previous request, I listed my reasons for disputing the information. I have enclosed it again and request that you reply within a reasonable amount of time.

Since this is my (SECOND, THIRD,FOURTH, ETC)) request, I will also be sending a copy of this letter to the Federal Trade Commission notifying them that I have signed receipts for letters sent to you and you have not complied with my request. I regret that I am being forced to take such action.

Please see my reasons for dispute below:

{dispute_item_and_explanation}

I also understand that you are required to notify me of your investigation results within 30 days and provide me with an updated copy of my credit report. My contact information is provided below.

Sincerely,

{client_signature}

_____

{client_first_name} {client_last_name}

Dispute Accounts That Should Be Included in BK

{client_first_name} {client_last_name}

{client_address}

{client_previous_address}

SS#: {client_social_security}

{credit_bureau)

{bureau_address}

{curr_date}

Re: (CREDIT REPORT NUMBER):

To Whom It May Concern,

The below account(s) should all show the following: included in bankruptcy. Accordingly, pursuant to the Fair Credit Reporting Act, please investigate and correct this inaccurate information.

{dispute_item_and_explanation}

Upon completion of this process, please mail an updated report to:

{client_first_name} {client_last_name}

{client_address}

{client_previous_address}

Sincerely,

{client_signature}

_____

{client_first_name} {client_last_name}

Validate Debt

{client_first_name} {client_last_name}

{client_address}

{bureau_address}

{curr_date}

To Whom It May Concern,

This letter is a formal complaint that you are reporting inaccurate and incomplete credit information.

I am distressed that you have included the information below in my credit profile and that you have failed to maintain reasonable procedures in your operations to assure maximum possible accuracy in the credit reports you publish. Credit reporting laws ensure that bureaus report only 100% accurate credit information. Every step must be taken to assure the information reported is completely accurate and correct. The following information therefore needs to be re-investigated.

{dispute_item_and_explanation}

I respectfully request to be provided proof of this alleged item, specifically the contract, note or other instrument bearing my signature.

Failing that, the item must be deleted from the report as soon as possible. The listed item is entirely inaccurate and incomplete, and as such represents a very serious error in your reporting. Please delete this misleading information and supply a corrected credit profile to all creditors who have received a copy within the last six months, or the last two years for employment purposes.

Additionally, please provide the name, address, and telephone number of each credit grantor or other subscriber.

Under federal law, you have thirty (30) days to complete your re-investigation. Be advised that the description of the procedure used to determine the accuracy and completeness of the information is hereby requested as well, to be provided within fifteen (15) days of the completion of your re-investigation.

Sincerely,

{client_signature}

_____

{client_first_name} {client_last_name}

Report Identity Theft

***************Instructions delete these before saving and sending***************

Fraud alerts are extremely helpful if you have been a victim of Identity theft. However, if you are NOT a victim of ID Theft, DO NOT place a fraud alert in your file as it serves no useful purpose.

***************Instructions delete these before saving and sending***************

{client_first_name} {client_last_name}

{client_address}

{bdate}

{ss_number}

{bureau_address}

Re: Identity Theft Notification

To Whom It May Concern,

This certified letter, receipt number_____ is to notify you that I believe I have been a victim of identity theft. Please rate the following accounts as "unrated" until this matter has been resolved.

I am formally requesting the following:

1) Please place a fraud alert note on my credit immediately.

2) Please notify all companies that have inquired in the past 12 months that identity theft has occurred.

3) Please do not authorize credit in my name without calling me first at ( ) _____ - _____ for verification.

4) Please send me a complete copy of my credit report as soon as possible so I can check it again for accuracy.

5) Please do not release my credit information to any credit issuer in the future without my permission.

I will inform you in writing when the matter has been resolved to remove the fraud alert. Enclosed is a copy of the police report (if you have one).

Kind regards,

{client_signature}

_____

{client_first_name} {client_last_name}

Report Identity Theft (Alternate)

**************Instructions delete these before saving and sending**************

Fraud alerts are very helpful if you have been a victim of ID theft. If you have not, do not place a fraud alert in your file as it serves no positive purpose.

**************Instructions delete these before saving and sending**************

{client_first_name} {client_last_name}

{client_address}

{t_no}

{bdate}

{ss_number}

{bureau_address}

Attention: Fraud Department

{curr_date}

Re: Identity Theft Notification

To Whom It May Concern,

I am a victim of identity theft and have enclosed a copy of my police report/identity theft report, a copy of my drivers license and social security card as proof of my identity, plus proof of my current address. I am writing to request that you place an immediate block on the following fraudulent information in my credit file within 4 days upon receipt of this correspondence.

I have recently obtained a copy of my credit file and the information does not relate to any transactions that I have made; therefore, I am requesting that these accounts be completely removed and blocked from my credit file. This is not a regular dispute I have filed a complaint with the Federal Trade Commission to document being a victim of identity theft.

Please block this fraudulent information per sections 605B, 615(f) and 623(a)(6) of the Fair Credit Reporting Act. I am requesting that the following fraudulent accounts be deleted and blocked from my credit file:

{dispute_item_and_explanation}

Kind regards,

{client_signature}

_____

{client_first_name} {client_last_name}

Enclosures: Police Report/Identity Theft Report, FCRA Sections 605B, 615(f), 623(a)(6)

Request to Merge Spouse's Credit History

{client_first_name} {client_last_name}

{client_address}

{bureau_address}

{curr_date}

To Whom It May Concern,

As my right by law, I am requesting that you merge my spouse's credit history with mine. Please make the necessary changes and forward a new copy of my updated credit report to me. Both my spouse and I have authorized this change.

My social security number: {ss_number}

My full name: {client_first_name} {client_middle_name} {client_last_name}

My address: {client_address} _

Spouses social security number:_____

Spouses full name:_____

My signature:_____

Spouses signature:_____

Regards,

{client_signature}

_____

{client_first_name} {client_last_name}

Request to Add Additional Credit Information

***************Instructions delete these before saving and sending***************

Getting positive information added by anyone other than the source is not an easy task. However, sometimes for a fee a Credit Bureau will often add the information if proof is acquired from the source. If you have valid proof of a debt with the creditor's name, contact information and history, include that with your request.

***************Instructions delete these before saving and sending***************

{client_first_name} {client_last_name}

{client_address}

{t_no}

{dob}

{ss_number}

{bureau_address}

Attention: Fraud Department

{curr_date}

Re: Request for Addition of Credit Information

To Whom It May Concern,

I am writing to request that you please include the additional information attached to my credit history report. You may verify this information with the source and I have included their contact details.

According to the Fair Credit Reporting Act (FCRA), Section 602(b), I am permitted to have accurate and true information reflected in my credit report. To accomplish this, I am requesting that my positive payment history with (Creditor's Name) be added. This will justly reflect my payment history. Therefore, I request that you immediately verify and add the enclosed payment history to my credit file. (Enclose proof from Creditor)

{dispute_item_and_explanation}

Please notify me within 30 days that the additional credit information has been added by sending an updated copy of my credit history report to my address above.The FCRA states "a consumer's credit report should reflect completeness and accuracy within a reasonable time after notification by the consumer." By adding this information to my records it will help to reflect a more accurate credit history report.If you require that this information be submitted to you directly from the source, please indicate the procedure and your fee to add this information.

Kind regards,

{client_signature}

_____

{client_first_name} {client_last_name}

Enclosures: Police Report/Identity Theft Report   FCRA Sections 605B, 615(f), 623(a)(6)

Credit Inquiry Removal Request

{client_first_name} {client_last_name}

{client_address}

{client_previous_address}

{bureau_address}

{curr_date}

RE: Request for Investigation of Unauthorized Inquiry

To Whom It May Concern,

I checked my personal credit report, which I acquired from your organization on (INSERT DATE OF REPORT) and I noticed that this unauthorized inquiry had been made:

{dispute_item_and_explanation}

I contacted (CREDITOR/FURNISHERS NAME), who placed the inquiry, and asked them to remove their credit inquiry from my credit profile. I also asked them to cease their illegal activities immediately, but to date there have been no responses from their office. Since sending the letter more than 30 business days ago, they have failed to respond and honor my request.

Therefore, I must request your help in resolving this matter. In accordance with the Fair Credit Reporting Act, I request you immediately initiate an investigation into this inquiry on my credit report to determine who authorized the inquiry. If, once your investigation is complete, you find my allegation to be true, please remove the unauthorized inquiry from my credit report and send me an updated copy of my credit report at my address listed above. If you do find the inquiry referenced above to be valid, I request that you please send me a full description of the procedures used in your investigation within 15 business days of the completion of the investigation.

Thank you for your help and assistance.

Sincerely,

{client_signature}

_____

{client_first_name} {client_last_name}

100 Word Consumer Statement

{client_first_name} {client_last_name}

{client_address}

{bureau_address}

Full Name: {client_first_name} {client_last_name}

{bdate}

{ss_number}

{client_address}

{t_no}

{client_previous_address}

{curr_date}

Re: Credit Report Number: (ENTER IF AVAILABLE) / Add Consumer Statement

To Whom It May Concern,

Please add following personal statement to my credit history report:

(YOUR 100 WORD (OR LESS) STATEMENT GOES HERE)

Enclosed are copies of documents identifying me by my name and address.

Thank you for your time and help in this matter.

Sincerely yours,

{client_signature}

_____

{client_first_name} {client_last_name}

Frivolous Dispute Response

{client_first_name} {client_last_name}

{client_address}

{t_no}

{bdate}

{ss_number}

{bureau_address}

{curr_date}

To Whom It May Concern,

I received a letter from your firm stating that my letter requesting verification of erroneous items on my report as being classified as "frivolous" or "irrelevant". I assure you that in no way do I consider a matter of such importance to me as frivolous nor irrelevant. In fact if you do not honor my original request to verify the items contained in my previous letter, mailed (DATE SENT) via certified mail, I will file a complaint with the Federal Trade Commission against your company.

I have included my original disputes for your convenience below:

The following information therefore needs to be reinvestigated. I respectfully request to be provided proof of this alleged item, specifically the contract, note or other instrument bearing my signature. Failing that, the items must be deleted from the report as soon as possible:

{dispute_item_and_explanation}

The listed item is completely inaccurate and incomplete, and is a very serious error in reporting. Please delete this misleading information, and supply a corrected credit profile to all creditors who have received a copy within the last 6 months, or the last 2 years for employment purposes.

Additionally, please provide the name, address, and telephone number of each credit grantor or other subscriber.

Under federal law, you have 30 days to complete your reinvestigation. Be advised that the description of the procedure used to determine the accuracy and completeness of the information is hereby requested as well. Please provide this information within 15 days of the completion of your reinvestigation.

Sincerely yours,

{client_signature}

{client_first_name} {client_last_name}

Frivolous Dispute Response (Alternate)

{client_first_name} {client_last_name}

{client_address}

{t_no}

{bdate}

{ss_number}

{bureau_address}

{curr_date}

To Whom It May Concern,

This letter is a formal complaint that you are reporting inaccurate and incomplete credit information. I am distressed that you have included the below information in my credit profile and have failed to maintain reasonable procedures in your operations to assure maximum possible accuracy in the credit reports you publish.

Credit reporting laws ensure that bureaus report only 100% accurate credit information. Every step must be taken to assure the information reported is completely accurate and correct.

The following information therefore needs to be reinvestigated. I respectfully request to be provided proof of this alleged item, specifically the contract, note or other instrument bearing my signature. Failing that, the items must be deleted from the report as soon as possible:

{dispute_item_and_explanation}

The listed item is completely inaccurate and incomplete, and is a very serious error in reporting. Please delete this misleading information, and supply a corrected credit profile to all creditors who have received a copy within the last 6 months, or the last 2 years for employment purposes.

Additionally, please provide the name, address, and telephone number of each credit grantor or other subscriber.

Under federal law, you have 30 days to complete your reinvestigation. Be advised that the description of the procedure used to determine the accuracy and completeness of the information is hereby requested as well. Please provide this information within 15 days of the completion of your reinvestigation.

Sincerely yours,

{client_signature}

_____

{client_first_name} {client_last_name}

Reply to Accusation of Credit Repair

***************Instructions delete these before saving and sending***************

Sometimes a Credit Bureau will accuse you of using a credit repair company (which is your right by law) Here is a letter to put them in their place and to avoid slowing down your disputes.

***************Instructions delete these before saving and sending***************

{client_first_name} {client_last_name}

{client_address}

{t_no}

{dob}

{ss_number}

{bureau_address}

Re: Credit Repair Accusation

To Whom It May Concern,

Please be advised that I have received your computer-generated letter stating that you have ceased investigation of my credit reports because, in your opinion, you believe that I have used a third party credit repair agency. Not only do I believe this to be a stall tactic on your part to grant you an additional 30 days to comply with my original request, but I believe it to be a blatant violation of the FCRA.

You were advised by me on (insert date) by certified mail (copy enclosed) that I questioned the accuracy of a few items on my credit reports. That request was written by me and mailed by me- not a third party agency. It appears obvious to me that you are abusing your power under the FCRA to escape a complete investigation.

Here again is the incorrect information being reported:

{dispute_item_and_explanation}

Additionally there is NO law that states a consumer cannot use a third party, so using that as your excuse is a irrelevant. In fact, the United States Congress has found the whole process so overwhelming that they afford consumers the right to use a third party on their behalf if the consumer so chooses. This is why your statement is so shameful.

I reserve the right to sue a credit bureau for violations of the Fair Credit Reporting Act and I believe I can prove that you did not use reasonable measures to insure the accuracy of my credit reports and now you are stalling the process even further.

I realize disputes can be expensive and it is your job to stall them, but you do so at great risk. Please take notice that this letter dated (insert today's date) is formal notice to you that I am requesting that you continue forward with my original investigation request and please send the results to me within 15 days. I therefore legally and lawfully refuse your "form letter" thus giving you only 15 days not 30 more.

I am annoyed and outraged at your accusation and I have researched my rights in regards to my credit file. Please expedite my original request immediately.

Sincerely yours,

{client_signature}

_____

{client_first_name} {client_last_name}

Debt Settlement Offer (Alternate)

{client_first_name} {client_last_name}

{client_address}

{creditor_name}

{creditor_address}

{creditor_city} {creditor_state} {creditor_zip}

{curr_date}

Re: Debtor's Settlement Offer for Account Number: {account_number}

To Whom It May Concern,

I am aware that I owe a balance to your company. This letter is an offer to settle the debt for less because of my inability to pay the full balance due to financial circumstances, because of: (LIST HARDSHIPS HERE), I am only able to pay a portion of this debt.

I realize you may be motivated as well, because of the age of the debt and my financial crisis. Refusing to work with me will only make matters worse for both of us.

You claim the amount owed on the account is $_____.

Please accept this offer to settle this account ONLY under the following conditions:

The parties involved agree to settle the account in full for the sum of $_____ and this amount is accepted as full and final payment on said debt. Complete discharge and settlement of all monies due will be created, provided that the amount agreed upon shall be paid in the following manner:

Payment terms: (i.e., 10 payments of $XXX on the 1st of each month after the execution of this agreement, 3 payments of $XXX to be paid monthly on the 1st of each month, 1 lump sum of $XXXX, etc.)

Payment location: (ADDRESS TO SEND THE PAYMENTS

Other terms: (list additional arrangements made, such as, creditor agrees to freeze the account without any additional fees or interest added to the balance, etc.) Credit reporting: (list status terms you are requesting such as "paid in full", "settled in full", "Paid as agreed", "settled for less", "deleted" etc.)

This agreement shall be binding under the laws of (LIST YOUR STATE AND THE CREDITOR'S STATE)

If your office agrees to this settlement, please send back confirmation on your company letterhead and signed by someone with the authority to accept such offers. Time is of the essence due to my present financial situation so please reply as soon as possible.

Sincerely,

{client_signature}

_____

{client_first_name} {client_last_name}

Intention to File FTC Complaint - After 30 Days

{client_first_name} {client_last_name}

{client_address}

{t_no}

{bdate}

{ss_number}

{bureau_address}

{curr_date}

To Whom It May Concern,

This letter shall serve as formal notice of my intent to file a complaint with the FTC, due to your blatant and objectionable disregard of the law.

As indicated by the attached copies of letters and mailing receipts, you have received and accepted through registered mail my dispute letter dated , as well as my follow-up letter dated . To date you have not done your duty as mandated by law. Your non-compliance with federal law is unacceptable, your disregard for it contemptible. Rest assured I shall hold you accountable.

Federal law requires you to respond within 30 days, yet you have failed to respond. Failure to comply with these federal regulations by credit reporting agencies are investigated by the Federal Trade Commission (see 15 USC 41, et seq.).I am maintaining a careful record of my communications with you on this matter; for the purpose of filing a complaint with the FTC should you continue in your non-compliance. I further remind you that, as in Wenger v. Trans Union Corp., No. 95-6445 (C.D.Cal. Nov. 14, 1995), you may be liable for your willful noncompliance.For the record, the following information is being erroneously included on my credit report, as I have advised you on two separate occasions, more than 75 days and again 40 days ago:

{dispute_item_and_explanation}

If you do not immediately remove this inaccurate and incomplete information, I will file a formal complaint with the Federal Trade Commission.

Should you continue to operate with complete disregard for the law, I intend to seek redress in civil action for recovery of damages, costs, and attorney fees. For this purpose I am carefully documenting these events, including the lack of response REQUIRED under law from you.Additionally, please provide the name, address, and telephone number of each credit grantor or other subscriber.Under federal law, you had 30 days to complete your re-investigation, yet you have failed to respond. Further delays are inexcusable.Be advised that the description of the procedure used to determine the accuracy and. completeness of the information is hereby requested as well, to be provided within 15 days of the completion of your re-investigation.

Sincerely,

{client_signature}

_____

{client_first_name} {client_last_name}

Intention to File FTC Complaint - After 30 Days (Alternate)

{client_first_name} {client_last_name}

{client_address}

{t_no}

{bdate}

{ss_number}

{bureau_address}

{curr_date}

To Whom It May Concern,

This letter is formal notice that you have failed to respond in a timely manner to my dispute letter of , deposited by registered mail with the U.S. Postal Service on that date.

Federal law requires you to respond within thirty (30) days, yet you have failed to respond. Failure to comply with these federal regulations by credit reporting agencies are investigated by the Federal Trade Commission (see 15 USC 41, et seq.). I am maintaining a careful record of my communications with you for the purpose of filing a complaint with the FTC should you continue in your non-compliance. I further remind you that, as in Wenger v. Trans Union Corp., No. 95-6445 (C.D.cal. Nov. 14, 1995), you may be liable for your willful non-compliance.

Be aware that I am making a final goodwill attempt to have you clear up this matter. You have 15 days to cure.

For your benefit, and as a gesture of my goodwill, I will restate my dispute. The following information needs to be verified and, following failure to verify, deleted from the report as soon as possible:

{dispute_item_and_explanation}

The listed item is entirely inaccurate and incomplete, and represents a very serious error in your reporting. Please delete this misleading information and supply a corrected credit profile to all creditors who have received a copy within the last six months, or the last two years for employment purposes.

Additionally, please provide the name, address, and telephone number of each credit grantor or other subscriber.

Under federal law you had thirty (30) days to complete your re-investigation, yet you have failed to respond. Do not delay any further.

Be advised that the description of the procedure used to determine the accuracy and completeness of the information is hereby requested as well, to be provided within fifteen (15).

Sincerely yours,

{client_signature}

_____

{client_first_name} {client_last_name}

Intention to File FTC Complaint - After 60 Days

{client_first_name} {client_last_name}

{client_address}

{bureau_address}

{curr_date}

To Whom It May Concern,

This letter shall serve as formal Notice of my Intent to file a Complaint with the FTC, due to your blatant disregard of the law.

As indicated by the attached copies of letters and mailing receipts, you have been delivered by registered mail both a dispute letter, dated 2/10/1999, as well as a follow-up letter, dated 3/20/1999. As of this moment, you have not done your duty mandated under the law. Your inaction in this matter is inexcusable, and your disregard for the law is contemptible. Rest assured, I will hold you to account.

As you are well aware, federal law requires you to respond within 30 days, yet you have failed to respond. Failure to comply with these federal regulations by credit reporting agencies are investigated by the Federal Trade Commission (see 15 USC 41, et seq.). I am maintaining a careful record of my communications with you on this matter, for the purpose of filing a complaint with the FTC should you continue in your non-compliance. I further remind you that, as in Wenger v. Trans Union Corp., No. 95-6445 (C.D.Cal. Nov. 14, 1995), you may be liable for your willful non-compliance.

For the record, the following information is being erroneously included on my credit report, as I have advised you on two separate occasions, more than 75 days and again 40 days ago:

{dispute_item_and_explanation}

If you do not immediately remove this inaccurate and incomplete information, I will file a formal complaint with the FTC. Furthermore, I intend to seek redress in civil action, for recover of damages, costs, and attorney's fees, should you continue in your deliberate obstruction of the law. For this purpose, I am carefully documenting these events, including the lack of response REQUIRED under law from you.

Additionally, please provide the name, address, and telephone number of each credit grantor or other subscriber.

Under federal law, you had 30 days to complete your re-investigation, yet you have failed to respond. Your continued delays are inexcusable.

Be advised that the description of the procedure used to determine the accuracy and completeness of the information is hereby requested as well, to be provided within 15 days of the completion of your re-investigation.

Sincerely yours,

{client_signature}

{client_first_name} {client_last_name}

Intent To File Lawsuit for FCRA Violation

{client_first_name} {client_last_name}

{client_address}

{client_previous_address}

SS# {client_social_security)

[Creditor Bureau]

[Address]

[City State Zip]

{curr_date}

Re: Intent To File Lawuit for FCRA Violation

To Whom It May Concern,

It is a crime to threaten lawsuit with no intention of doing so, therefore you can take heed that I am very serious about filing suit against your company. I have sent (NUMBER OF LETTERS) previous letters to you, all by certified mail (receipts enclosed) requesting that you remove inaccurate information from my file and you have failed to do so.

Accordingly, I can show a judge that these accounts are inaccurate and that you violated the Fair Credit Reporting Act by ignoring my requests to investigate the items. My previous letters (all sent by certified mail) stated my reasons for an investigation and these reasons were not frivolous in any way.

If this final request does not prompt you to conduct a proper investigation of these accounts in question, and send proof to me of said investigation, I will file a civil suit in my county for damages and you can travel to defend yourself.

I take my credit very serious and your lack of professionalism and assistance disappoints me. I am well aware of my rights under the Fair Credit Reporting Act and I intend to pursue them to the maximum.

I await your response.

Sincerely,

{client_signature}

_____

{client_first_name} {client_last_name}

cc: Federal Trade Commission; Attorney General

Dispute Collections

{client_first_name} {client_last_name}

{client_address}

{creditor_name}

{creditor_address}

{creditor_city}, {creditor_state} {creditor_zip}

{curr_date}

Re: Dispute of Collections Action: Case # {account_number}.

[If a collection agency has sent written notice, your case number is likely in the letter. If you have not received a written notice from the collection agency, tailor this line accordingly. For example, show the date you were contacted by the collection agency and/or identify the creditor by name if you can.]

To [person whose name appears on agency's notice to you]:

On [date] I was contacted by [name of person who called you] of your agency, who informed me that [name of collection agency] is attempting to collect [amount of claimed debt]. This individual is collecting on behalf of [name of creditor]. [OR] This individual would not tell me for whom you are supposed to be collecting.

[OR]

On [date] I received a written notice of the claimed debt, a copy of which is attached.

This is to inform you that I dispute the debt because [insert reason for dispute, e.g. the agency has mistaken you with someone else or the debt has been paid. Include copies, not originals, of any correspondence that support your dispute]. I am hereby requesting that you confirm the fact that I owe this debt as required by any applicable state and federal laws. Please contact the creditor to obtain verification.

In addition, under the provisions of state and federal Fair Debt Collection Practices Act (FDCPA), Fair Credit Reporting Act (FCRA), and related consumer statutes, I am hereby instructing you to cease collection of the debt while efforts are made to obtain verification. Until you resolve this error with the creditor, you should neither contact me nor anyone else except the creditor about this collection.

Furthermore, any reporting of this matter to credit reporting agencies is premature. Until you have investigated my dispute, you should not relay negative information to a credit reporting agency. If negative information has already been reported, you must notify the agency to remove said report until the investigative process is over so that my credit report remains accurate, or at the very least, my credit report should be updated to reflect my dispute.

Your next contact with me should be to either notice that the creditor has failed to provide verification of the debt and that the matter has been closed or that you believe that this debt is valid and are providing proof of my responsibility. If the former, please confirm that I am not being held responsible for the debt in writing and also that if the account has already been noted on my credit report, that you will contact the bureau(s) in question to have the account removed. If the latter, I expect that you will provide me with an explanation as to why you have decided not to remove this account from collections and a copy of all documents relevant to the debt such as the application, bills, records of communications and payments, and any other data that indicates my responsibility.

I am instructing you not to contact any third parties such as my employer, neighbors, friends or family members. In addition, you may not contact me by phone at work or at my home about this collection activity. All future correspondence should be sent to me in writing.

[If you wish to still speak to a collector by phone, indicate the times when it is okay to contact you or note the name, address, and phone number of your attorney, if you have retained one.]

Please acknowledge that you have received this notice by [Pick a date that is two weeks from date of letter].

Sincerely,

{client_signature}

_____

{client_first_name} {client_last_name}

Temporarily Stop Collections

{client_first_name} {client_last_name}

{client_address}

(Name of Collection Agency)

{creditor_address}

{creditor_city}, {creditor_state} {creditor_zip}

{curr_date}

To [person whose name appears on agency's notice to you]:

Thank you for your recent inquiry. This is not a refusal to pay, but a notice that your claim is being disputed. This is a request for validation made pursuant to the Fair Debt Collection Practices Act.

Be advised that I am not requesting a "verification" that you have my mailing address, I am requesting a "validation;" that is, competent evidence that I have some contractual obligation to pay you.

You should also be aware that sending unsubstantiated demands for payment through the United States Mail System might constitute mail fraud under federal and state law. You may wish to consult with a competent legal advisor before your next communication with me.

Your failure to satisfy this request within the requirements of the Fair Debt Collection Practices Act will be construed as your absolute waiver of any and all claims against me, and your tacit agreement to compensate me for costs and attorney fees.

Sincerely,

{client_signature}

{client_first_name} {client_last_name}

Cease and Desist

{client_first_name} {client_last_name}

{client_address}

(Collection Agency)

{creditor_address}

{creditor_city}, {creditor_state} {creditor_zip}

Attn: (PERSON OR DEPARTMENT THAT CONTACTED YOU)

{curr_date}

Re: Notice to Cease Contact, Case # (ENTER CASE NUMBER IF AVAILABLE, PLUS CREDITOR INFORMATION AND ACCOUNT NUMBER)

To (PERSON WHOSE NAME APPEARS ON THE AGENCY'S NOTICE TO YOU):

(CHOOSE ONE)

Since approximately _____, I have received several phone calls and letters from you concerning an overdue account with the above-named creditor.

(OR)

On (date) I received written notice of the claimed debt, a copy of which is attached.

This is to give you notice to cease all contact with me or anyone else except the creditor about this claimed debt. Accordingly, under 15 U.S.C. Sec. 1692c, this is my formal notice to you to cease all further communications with me. If you must contact me, please do so in writing and not by telephone.

I look forward to your acknowledgement that you have received this notice by [insert a date that is two weeks from the date of this letter].

Sincerely,

{client_signature}

_____

{client_first_name} {client_last_name}

Cease and Desist (Alternate)

{client_first_name} {client_last_name}

{client_address}

{client_previous_address}

{creditor_name}

{creditor_address}

{creditor_city} {creditor_state} {creditor_zip}

{creditor_phone}

{curr_date}

Re: Account # {account_number}

To Whom It May Concern,

Pursuant to my rights under federal debt collection laws, I am requesting that you cease and desist communication with me, as well as my family, friends or my employer, in relation to this or any other alleged debts you claim I owe.

You are hereby notified that if you do not comply with this request, I will immediately file a complaint with the Federal Trade Commission and the Attorney General of [your state here]. Civil and criminal claims will also be pursued.

Sincerely,

{client_signature}

_____

{client_first_name} {client_last_name}

Cease and Desist (Alternate 2)

{client_first_name} {client_last_name}

{client_address}

{client_previous_address}

{creditor_name}

{creditor_address}

{creditor_city} {creditor_state} {creditor_zip}

{creditor_phone}

{curr_date}

Re: Account # {account_number}

To Whom It May Concern,

You are hereby notified under provisions of Public Laws 95-109 and 99-361, also known as the Fair Debt Collection Practices Act, that your services are no longer desired.

Immediately cease and desist all attempts to collect the above debt. Failure to comply with this law will result in my immediately filing a complaint with the Federal Trade Commission and the Attorney General of [your state here]. Civil and criminal claims will also be pursued against you and your company.

Let this letter also serve as your warning that I may utilize telephone recording devices in order to document any telephone conversations that we may have in the future.

Furthermore, if any negative information is placed on my credit bureau reports by your agency after receipt of this notice, this will cause me to file suit against you and your organization, both personally and corporately, to seek any and all legal remedies available to me by law.

It is my policy neither to recognize nor deal with collection agencies, and I will only settle this account with the original creditor.

Sincerely,

{client_signature}

_____

{client_first_name} {client_last_name}

Complaint about Harassment

{client_first_name} {client_last_name}

{client_address}

{creditor_name}

{creditor_address}

{creditor_city}, {creditor_state} {creditor_zip}

{curr_date}

Name(s) on account: Test Test test

Account number: {account_number}

Date loan/debt incurred: (DATE)

Original loan/debt amount: (ORIGINAL AMOUNT OF LOAN/DEBT)

Amount past due: (AMOUNT CURRENTLY PAST DUE)

Re: Collection agency: {creditor_name}

To Whom It May Concern:

I have been unable to pay the full amount of the loan/debt noted above for the following reason(s):

(ENTER REASONS HERE)

Although I have an outstanding debt, I have the right to be treated by a collection agency with dignity and respect. The collection agency you've hired (as noted above), however, has engaged in the following practices which violate the federal Fair Debt Collection Practices Act:

(ENTER COLLECTION AGENCY MISCONDUCT HERE)

I am willing to forego the legal remedies I have available, including a lawsuit in small claims court seeking punitive damages against you and the agency, in exchange for your written promise to permanently cease all efforts to collect this debt and remove all negative entries regarding this debt from my credit file. I expect to hear from you immediately.

Sincerely,

{client_signature}_____

{client_first_name} {client_last_name}

cc: Federal Trade Commission   State Collection Agency Licensing Board   Collection Agency: (NAME OF OFFENDING COLLECTION AGENCY)

Warning of VOD refusal and FDCPA violations

{client_first_name} {client_last_name}

{client_address}

{creditor_name}

{creditor_address}

{creditor_city} {creditor_state} {creditor_zip}

{curr_date}

Re: {account_number}

To Whom It May Concern,

Please be apprised that you are in direct violation of the Fair Debt Collections Practices Act. In my opinion you have violated at least three sections of this act by:

Failing to validate a debt as allowed to the debtor under 15 USC 1692 (g) Section 809 (b)

Communicating with a debtor after receiving a cease and desist certified mail under 15 USC 1692 (g) Section 805 (c)

Harassment of alleged debtor under the "abuse & harassment" subsection of the statute, USC 1692 (g) Section 806 (5)

I have complete and thorough records of your violations and I am prepared to protect myself and my rights from unscrupulous collection agencies.

In (EXACT DATE), I sent by certified mail (receipt number: (CERTIFIED MAIL RECEIPT NUMBER), a request for your office to provide me with proof and evidence of the debt you alleged I owed, and I did so within 30 days of receiving your first notice. In that same letter I also included my cease and desist instructions.

After verified delivery of my letter (via your office's signature), you proceeded to mail a simple bill which is NOT considered a "validation of debt" by any means. You may wish to familiarize yourself with what is required when validating a debt.

Your office also proceeded to contact me by phone after the delivery and acceptance of my certified letter. Contacting a person after a cease and desist can lead to serious trouble for your agency including damages of up to $1000.00 per incident.

I highly doubt that this $(ENTER AMOUNT OF DEBT) debt is worth your agency's license and the fees and penalties for violations of the FDCPA.

There is no question that you willfully violated my rights and that I could bring charges against you immediately. However, I am assuming this has been a terrible mistake on your part and that you will take appropriate steps to enlighten yourself and your staff of such dangerous actions.

I will also be checking my credit report to see if you have willfully reported an unverified and disputable debt to the credit bureaus. If so, that will be a violation of the Fair Credit Reporting Act. I will state again in this certified mailing that you have failed to verify the debt as accurate, you have provided no proof of this alleged debt, and I must remind you again to not contact me in any way via phone or mail in reference to collecting this debt.

If I receive anything other than absolute proof from you, provided by the original creditor, I will assume you are harassing me and ignoring my cease and desist, and I will take action against you for these continued violations and abuse.

Sincerely,

{client_signature}

_____

{client_first_name} {client_last_name}

Warning Violation for Expired Debt Collection

{client_first_name} {client_last_name}

{client_address}

{creditor_name}

{creditor_address}

{creditor_city} {creditor_state} {creditor_zip}

{curr_date}

Re: {account_number}

To Whom It May Concern,

Please be advised that you are attempting to collect on an expired debt. I am invoking my right to cease you, based on factual law that this debt in question is legally expired under the Statute of Limitations. Accordingly, I am requesting that you do not attempt to collect this expired debt, and should you seek legal recourse I will invoke my right of the expired statute as a valid defense.

Additionally any attempts to harm my credit history and rating by updating or changing dates after you have been informed that the debt is expired, is a direct violation of the FDCPA. Any abuse to my credit rating on your part will be met with all recourse available to me by the law.

I am aware of how long items may remain on my credit reports and any attempt to extend the reporting time will be investigated by me, and reported to my State Attorney General and the American Collectors Association. I am completely aware of how long the debt may be legally collectable and how long it may be legally reportable. I realize a debt is allowed to be reported on my credit history for no longer than 7 years, and my research has shown me that often a collection agency will reset the date of original charge off to the date they purchased it, thus trying to extend the reporting time in an attempt to force a consumer into paying it. I am informing you of this knowledge so that you may do the right thing.

I have no intentions of renewing the expired statute of limitations, so please stop wasting your time contacting me. I expect this will be the last time I hear from you.

Sincerely,

{client_signature}

_____

{client_first_name} {client_last_name}

Warning Violation for Expired Debt Collection (Alternate)

{client_first_name} {client_last_name}

{client_address}

{creditor_name}

{creditor_address}

{creditor_city} {creditor_state} {creditor_zip}

{curr_date}

Re: {account_number}

To Whom It May Concern,

Please be advised that you are attempting to collect on an expired debt. I am invoking my right to cease you, based on factual law that this debt in question is legally expired under the Statute of Limitations. Accordingly, I am requesting that you do not attempt to collect this expired debt, and should you seek legal recourse I will invoke my right of the expired statute as a valid defense.

Additionally any attempts to harm my credit history and rating by updating or changing dates after you have been informed that the debt is expired, is a direct violation of the FDCPA. Any abuse to my credit rating on your part will be met with all recourse available to me by the law.

I am aware of how long items may remain on my credit reports and any attempt to extend the reporting time will be investigated by me, and reported to my State Attorney General and the American Collectors Association.

I am completely aware of how long the debt may be legally collectable and how long it may be legally reportable. I realize a debt is allowed to be reported on my credit history for no longer than 7 years, and my research has shown me that often a collection agency will reset the date of original charge off to the date they purchased it, thus trying to extend the reporting time in an attempt to force a consumer into paying it. I am informing you of this knowledge so that you may do the right thing.

I have no intentions of renewing the expired statute of limitations, so please stop wasting your time contacting me. I expect this will be the last time I hear from you.

Sincerely,

{client_signature}

_____

{client_first_name} {client_last_name}

Warning of Expired Statute of Limitations

{client_first_name} {client_last_name}

{client_address}

{creditor_name}

{creditor_address}

{creditor_city} {creditor_state} {creditor_zip}

{curr_date}

RE: Account number {account_number}

To Whom It May Concern,

Please be advised that you are attempting to collect on an expired debt. I am invoking my right to cease you, based on factual law that this debt in question is legally expired under the Statute of Limitations.

Accordingly, I am requesting that you do not attempt to collect this expired debt, and should you seek legal recourse I will invoke my right of the expired statute as a valid defense.

Additionally any attempts to harm my credit rating by updating or changing dates after you have been informed that the debt is expired, are a direct violation of the FDCPA.

Any abuse to my credit rating on your part will be met with all recourse available to me.

I am aware of how long items may remain on my credit reports and any attempt to extend the reporting time will be investigated by me, and reported to the American Collectors Association and my State Attorney General.

I am completely aware of how long the debt is legally collectable and how long it is legally reportable. I realize a debt is allowed to be reported to my credit for 7 years, and my research has shown me that often a collection agency will reset the date of original charge off to the date they purchased it, thus trying to extend the reporting time in an attempt to force a consumer into paying it. I am informing you of this knowledge so that you may do the right thing.

I have no intention of renewing the expired statute of limitations, so please stop wasting your time contacting me.

I expect this will be the last time I hear from you.

Sincerely,

{client_signature}_____

{client_first_name} {client_last_name}

Made in the USA
Columbia, SC
03 March 2019